A Primer on School Budgeting

Robert N. Kratz, Charles A. Scott, and Harry T. Zechman

The Scarecrow Press, Inc.
A Scarecrow Education Book
Lanham, Maryland, and London
2001
Originally published 1998
Technomic Publishing Company, Inc.
Lancaster, Pennsylvania

SCARECROW PRESS, INC.
A Scarecrow Education Book

Published in the United States of America
by Scarecrow Press, Inc.
4720 Boston Way, Lanham, Maryland 20706
www.scarecrowpress.com

4 Pleydell Gardens, Folkestone
Kent CT20 2DN, England

The Technomic edition of this book was catalogued as follows by the Library of Congress:
Main entry title:
A Primer on School Budgeting
A Technomic Publishing Company book
Bibliography: p.
Includes index p. 147

Library of Congress Catalog Card No. 98-60467
ISBN: 156676-639-7
Reprinted by Scarecrow Education

∞™ The paper used in this publication meets the minimum requirements of American National Standard for Information Sciences—Permanence of Paper for Printed Library Materials, ANSI/NISO Z39.48–1992.
Manufactured in the United States of America.

Table of Contents

Preface

SCHOOL district budgeting is a daunting process. Budgets themselves are intimidating. They run to eight or more figures, are subject to much scrutiny, and tend to be complicated, even convoluted. Beginning school administrators, often prepared with only one rather theoretical course on the subject, view the budget development process as a nightmare from which they may not awaken. Teachers and board members who have little experience with budgeting also are justifiably concerned by the prospect of their involvement in budgeting.

This book is written as a practical manual on the budget development process for administrators, board members, and teachers who are not as knowledgeable on the subject as they feel they need to be.

The first two chapters are designed to assist the reader with background for the more practical chapters that follow. The subtopics in Chapter 1 show readers that budgeting is and should be a goal-oriented planning process. It should convince him or her that budgeting is necessarily planning and that planning is the most common thread running through all aspects and levels of school administration, and most certainly including fiscal management. Chapters 1 and 2's components are arranged in order for apparent logic, flow, or chronology in the process. The first two chapters provide the reader with resources to better understand and use Chapters 3 through 5.

Although the subtopics of Chapter 2 are more theoretical than the following chapters, they are practical aids for viewing the very pragmatic text and examples of the last three chapters of the book. For example, problems encountered by those assigned to build the budget—problems such as the negative aspects of budget development, the difficulty in providing vision while considering history, or the perennial and career-threatening issues associated with communications or the lack thereof—are presented here as advisory backdrop.

What follows in Chapters 3 through 5 are descriptions of how a budget is put together, approved, and used. These process stages are meant to be descriptive, not directions to the only way to develop a budget. The authors are in agreement not directions to the only way to develop a budget. The authors are in agreement on budgetary philosophy but are aware of and experienced with many variations on the specifics of actual budgeting.

Chapters 3, 4, and 5 of this book, although based on the points made initially in the first two chapters, are more experientially derived and, consequently, have fewer references to scholarly works from more theoretical points of view.

Some of the topics covered here will not necessarily be part of every well-developed budget, for example, the long-range maintenance plan or ideas on privatizing. However, three themes are established early in the book, and attention is called to them throughout:

- Budgeting is planning.
- Administration in budgeting is necessary leadership.
- Communication, of necessity, pervades all aspects of budget development.

Acknowledgments

THE authors wish to acknowledge the contributions of the following, all of whom helped make this book better: Kay Bailey, Thomas A. Baum, James A. Dilorio, Paul Kelly, Dr. Janet Smith, and Joan Steiner.

We also wish to recognize and thank our wives, Ann, Jacquelyn, and Robin, who supported us in this project from the start.

CHAPTER 1

Planning a Budget Development Process: Theoretical Bases

PURPOSES OF THE BUDGET

THIRTY-FIVE years ago in their now classic *Budgeting for Better Schools* Ovsiew and Castetter saw the purposes of a budget as:

> Giving an account of financial stewardship
> Facilitating control of expenditures
> Identifying key elements in the management of funds, facilities, and personnel
> Appraising the operation of the school program
> Specifying educational objectives in financial plans.[1]

More recently described purposes can be seen in Hartman's *School District Budgeting*.[2] He writes that budgeting is for planning, public review and approval, justification of public funds expenditure, control, and fiscal performance evaluation.

Budgeting, then, provides the public school district with a planning process that is of great practical value to the staff and administration all year and prompts planning in other areas—curriculum, purchasing, facility maintenance, and development. For example,

- assessment of need and goal determination
- program evaluation
- required approval of the recommended revenue and expenditure plan
- expenditure justification and control
- evaluation of fiscal performance

Thorough and sensible budgeting will provide vehicles for achieving these purposes but certainly not automatically. If administrators choose to ignore the tenets of good management or leadership, budgeting will not serve its purposes. As pointed out below, budgeting is a planning process. If the administration does not make evaluation a functioning part of the plan, for example, the resulting budget won't serve its purposes. Budgeting is hardly a turn-key operation. It does require some administrative skill.

BUDGETING AS EDUCATIONAL LEADERSHIP

Leadership is having a vision, setting goals, providing direction, planning, organizing, and allocating resources, among other things. Successful leaders demonstrate ability in these areas, but budgeting also requires these abilities. Educational leaders responsible for the budgeting process, or parts of it, must exert leadership by sharing their vision for the organization, by establishing and communicating goals, and by making plans for the future realization of their vision and goals. They have to establish organization and communicate ideas, plans, and concepts of allocation and control. They must provide direction. The budget development process requires this kind of leadership.

"Leaders must create for their institutions clear cut and measurable goals based on advice from all elements of the community. They must be allowed to proceed without being crippled by bureaucratic machinery that saps their strength, energy, and initiative."—Warren Bennis, *Why Leaders Can't Lead*[3]

Cattanach[4] points out that leadership is easier to recognize than to define but goes on to say that, "effective leadership articulates commonly held values and beliefs, develops shared commitments to common goals, and inspires others to do what they ordinarily wouldn't do." The latter supports the concept of budgeting being viewed as leadership. Budgeting is and should be goal oriented. Yet given the times in which we live, it is often difficult for educational leaders to develop, communicate, and adhere to the goals that stem from their values and beliefs. But that is what leadership is all about. Leadership is identifying belief-based goals for the organization and then enabling the organization to meet those goals. Educators in leadership positions must assure that vision is translated into goals and that the school then meets those goals. The budget development process and the resultant budget are tools in translating vision into reality. The leader who envisions increased student opportunity or better student facilities or higher levels of educational quality uses the budgeting process to lead toward the reality he or she sees as translations of that vision.

"A foolish consistency is the hobgoblin of little minds adored by little statesmen and philosophers and divines. With consistency a great soul has simply nothing to do. . . . Speak what you think now in hard words and tomorrow speak what tomorrow thinks in hard words again, though it contradicts every thing you said today."—R. W. Emerson,

Warren Bennis writes, "Change is the metaphysics of our age."[5] Change today is constant and all-pervasive. Therefore, it must be dealt with by any leader in a process as fundamental as budgeting. The budget process is also a tool for dealing with change, but it is a leadership tool, not a mechanical or mindless aid. Leaders have to lead in budgeting or the budget will be merely a compilation of numbers with little or no meaning for the future.

In an article entitled "Budgeting Advice for Newcomers to the Superintendency," Graczyk and Godshall describe a number of budgeting techniques for the new superintendent, two of which are noted here. They advise the new superintendent to "maintain the existing budgeting process for at least one complete fiscal year," thereby fully understanding the existing process and, consequently, being able to implement meaningful, needed change. In addition, they admonish the new administrator against "unrealistic fiscal promises" made in the budgeting process.[6] Leadership is planned, constructive, needed change rather than change for the sake of change. The new administrator should not be making changes merely because he/she is the new administrator.

One final aspect of leadership must be mentioned here: determination. Although it may be a part of the makeup of any leader, determination is particularly important in educational budgetary leadership, given the trend of the times. Educational leaders today are called upon to be dedicated advocates of children, to resolutely pursue progressive ideas, and to constantly seek out sources of school improvement. School leaders have an obligation to budget with a determination that underscores the importance of what they advocate.

Fussing and whining are not leadership or even determination. All too often the nominal educational leader finds him/herself in a position of defeat at the hands of a higher level in the organization on a budgetary issue important to him/her and mistakenly tries to fuss or whine his/her way to success. This "beating a dead horse" rarely turns the collective head of the board or changes the mind of the superintendent. You would be better served to return to the field on a later day. If your pet project doesn't get into this year's budget, continued fussing and whining won't change much. It won't lead to your becoming a real leader, and it could lead to your ceasing to be even a nominal leader. It is better to return next year armed for effective persuasion (fussing and whining aren't persuasion, either).

BUDGETING AS PLANNING

"No one plans to fail; they only fail to plan."—Old saying of unknown origin, perhaps pre-Columbian graffiti

---

Several definitions of planning should be instructive here. Galbraith's definition is practical but from an industrial model: "foreseeing the action between initiation of production and its completion and preparing for the accomplishments of these actions."[7] Castetter and Burchell's definition pertains to education: "Planning in regard to the educational program may be defined as deciding in advance what the goals will be, what learning experiences are needed to achieve the goals, how these experiences will be organized, and what services will be provided."[8] The educational planning dissertation from which the above two definitions were drawn developed the following definition and assumed, among other things, that educational planning is an administrative function:

> Educational planning is an attempt to foresee a desired and improved future for education, or some phase of it, through a continuous, rational and systematic process of advanced decision making and commitment of resources. Alternatives are arranged and selected in setting goals and policy in order that the best knowledge of the environment available be used in assuring that the future that is desired comes about.[9]

The latter fairly defines planning in education, and it also fairly describes budgeting.

"Other forms of life have shown themselves capable of myriad adaptations to their varied, changing, and complex environments; but man aspires to control his future; hence planning whose powerful appeal depends on its promise to harness destiny."—Aaron Wildavsky, *Budgeting: A Comparative Theory of Budgetary Process*[10]

Planning is an effort to ameliorate the difficulties in foreseeing and coping with the future. It offers direction while providing some measure of performance.

It is an attempt to identify and take appropriate risks. It forces higher-level thinking and research rather than chance or hunches. Planning also aids in the competition for money and other scarce resources. It helps schools to accommodate rapid growth and to capitalize on their strengths. Finally, planning increases an administrator's span of control and potential as a leader.[11]

Budgetary planning, particularly in education, involves numerous people, some who are not administrators and some who are not even educators. Budgetary planning is unquestionably a positive, higher-order, directive skill, which is part of the leadership that administrators are expected to provide.

Chapter 6 of Hack, Candoli, and Ray's *School Business Administration: A Planning Approach* is entitled "Planning and Budgeting." In this chapter the authors contend that educational planning "is the essential feature of effective budgeting in the schools."[12] They make several other planning-related points worthy of note here. They recommend that the superintendent be the chief planner regardless of the planning methods used by the district. However, they visualize planning as pervasive in all district functions, and they see methods and capacities for planning as individual to each district.[13] Finally, they note that the very process of budgeting "requires a kind of orderly planning that otherwise might never take place. Budgeting, then, forces the community, board, administrators, and staff to plan together what needs to be done, how it will be done and by whom it will be done."[14]

BUDGETING AS A PROCESS

Webster defines "process" as "a series of activities or operations definitively conducing to an end." Budgeting is, or at least should be, a dynamic, ongoing, almost organic series of activities. It is hard to imagine it as static or a single event. To be effective, budgeting must occur over time and lead to a desired product through multiple activities or operations. The product is not the budget document, however, as much as it is the improved educational program of the district.

As noted in the earlier section on the purposes of budgeting, it also can be seen from the phases of budgeting (Figure 1.1) that budgeting is a series of activities or operations. It must be noted, however, that some phases, such as appraisal/evaluation, communication, and implementation, in particular, are not single points in time but, rather, periods, and in some instances long periods. For example, communications, as will be stressed later, is a phase that pervades the entire budget development process.

Like many other processes, the budget process is as important as the result. It is clear when viewing the various aspects of budget development that not merely the resultant budget but planning, goal setting, participatory decision making, and the like are very valuable also.

Appraisal/evaluation
Needs assessment
Cost analysis
Revenue estimates
Drafting
Preapproval
Adoption
Communication
Implementation

Figure 1.1 Phases of the budgeting process.

GOAL-ORIENTED BUDGETING

School people have always had more ideas, wants, and needs than their budgets could pay for, and funding of schools hasn't gotten any easier over time. One way of dealing with increasing wants and needs coupled with decreasing or, at the very least, non-increasing sources of funds is setting goals and prioritizing them. Although it may seem obvious that setting goals for your school entity and then prioritizing the goals for funding as finances permit is a logical management concept, there is also scholarly support for it.

America's system of thirteen years of free public education for its youngsters is not without cost. That cost is both financial, in the form of taxation, and contentious, in the form of governmental bickering, buck passing, arrogance, and obfuscation. Much of the latter is related to attempts to avoid levying the former.

Although education in this country is a state responsibility, it is delegated to local municipalities or school districts (except in Hawaii). Jordan and Lyons tell us that,

> Provisions for financing public schools involve several interactive policy decisions: appropriation of funds by state legislatures, adoption of district budgets by local boards of education, and assessment and collection of county property taxes. These are state and local decisions. Often state efforts to provide equality in funding are thwarted because of the context of the local and state political environment in which school funding decisions are made.
>
> In the political environment, legislators are confronted with competing demands from local school districts as well as from public agencies. These competing demands often result in decisions that are not made on a rational basis of cost effectiveness or on a basis of equity, which gives students equal access to educational services. Thus political expediency often leads legislators to make decisions resulting in short term solutions rather than decisions that over the long term are more educationally and economically sound. It is within this context that governors and legislators must grapple to find ways to fund schools that are both adequate and equitable.[15]

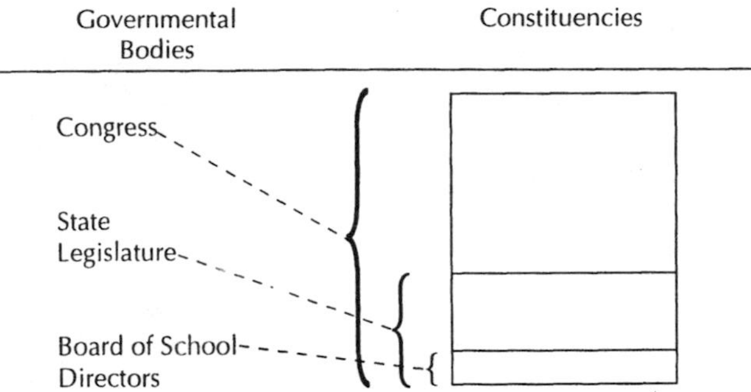

Figure 1.2 Government interactions.

Jordan and Lyons further inform us that in the last 20 years, local, state, and federal policy makers have had increasing difficulty when making decisions relative to policy goals for financing schools.[16] Again, these policy decisions don't take place in a vacuum. They are interactive. All three levels of government interact with each other, and, moreover, their respective constituencies are part of each other (Figure 1.2). Social and economic issues at all three levels are also interactive, further complicating the already difficult process of school funding.

All of this consternation cries out for enlightened decision making at all three levels but most assuredly calls for goal setting by local school districts as a part of budget development. Schools can defend against this morass of intergovernmental squabbling and constituencies at odds with one another by setting goals that take into account the various component interactions as they prepare to develop their budgets. Better yet, they can be proactive on their own behalf by setting goals that provide vision and direction to their budget development.

Goal setting also relates the budgeted activities to the district's mission. See Figures 1.3 as well as Figures 2.5 and 2.6 for examples of how two districts approach relating goals to mission. Also see the budget example at the end of the book. Note that the goals themselves, or at least through their objectives/activities, should be measurable. Also note that goals that are part of budgeting must be costed out, and the costs of each included in that budget.

BUDGETING AS A DEMOCRATIC PROCESS

PARTICIPATION BY THOSE AFFECTED

In a book describing the school superintendency in terms of leadership, Davidson writes, "The most important reason for staff participation in decision

Promote multicultural education and, therefore, understanding in an increasingly diverse school community

- Advertise faculty and administrative vacancies and district's interest in multicultural understanding at 200 colleges/ universities and recruit at three job fairs/year ($600)
- The curriculum committee will analyze the K–12 curriculum and recommend to the board needed additional courses and activities
- The administration will examine practices and procedures to identify those that may deter multiculturalism

Provide appropriate K–12 computer instruction

- Make needed revisions in the district computer plan
- Update computer education plan, including staff development, by February
- Recommend next steps to the board for inclusion in budget under development ($130,000)

. . .

Projected hard costs for budget being developed are in parentheses.

Figure 1.3 Budgeting goals and concomitant objectives/activities.

making is that better decisions usually result."[17] The participatory decision-making "process produces higher-quality decisions which are more likely to be supported." Davidson also points out that staff involvement in decision making is virtually a reality.[18]

The latter is particularly true in budget development, probably due to the quality of results, but also due to schools being operated at the local government level in the American democratic tradition. It is now conventional for school boards to develop budgets in the sunshine of public scrutiny by those most directly affected, not by just the superintendent, although certainly he or she provides the leadership.

Budgets are no longer put together by a few administrators and routinely adopted by rubber-stamp boards, nor should they be. Current conventional wisdom and our representative democracy demand that those affected by what is ultimately adopted have input in the process. This seems particularly pertinent relative to the tools needed to meet the goals of the schools and to the challenges issued them by the communities they serve.

OPENNESS AND COMMUNICATION

Democracy and, in most cases, the law also call for an openness and a greater level of communication, which is also in keeping with current views abhorring secrecy on the part of the schools. Assuredly today, if not in the past, school people must be open about what they have and have not included in any budget. The school board's constituency may not have a need or right to know how much money is in a budget to settle on-going faculty collective bargaining, but reserves for most other contingencies are to be public knowledge. Likewise, the anticipated costs of that new reading program or additional interscholastic sport should be openly communicated to the school community as part of the budget development process (see Budget Example).

VISION AND HISTORY

Vision is cited above as an element of leadership. It is necessary here to further develop the notion of vision relative to history, as the two can appear to be conflicting, if not mutually exclusive, in the budgeting process. Even if incremental budgeting (described in the next section) is minimized, budgeting is still somewhat of an historically based process. Budget developers cannot easily ignore, nor should they, local budgeting history or historical state and national governmental positions. Vision, too, is an aspect of the budget development process or should be.

Leadership has to be forward looking while engaged in budgetary planning. It cannot ignore history, but it should not dwell on it. Educational leaders should not be forced to relive history, although they may consciously choose to.

"Teachers and administrators seek to understand their superintendent's vision in part because they truly want to contribute to its realization. A worthy vision orients constituents, enabling them to organize their joint efforts."—Susan Johnson, *Leading to Change*[19]

Early in the budget development process as part of the assessment of needs, budgeting leaders must envision the programs they want and need,[20] not only for content but also for quality, not only for the near term but also for the future. The vision expected of leaders in education includes envisioning directions in which the schools should be moving and then using the budget to help move them there.

"Teachers and administrators look to their leaders for reassurance that their district is moving ahead rather than falling behind or standing still." —Susan Johnson[21]

TYPES OF BUDGETING

The following are descriptive summaries of the major types of budgeting, including the pluses and minuses of each. Rarely will one see pure examples of any of these; rather, most budgeting is a variation on one or more of these themes.

INCREMENTAL BUDGETING

"Historically the most common technique by which districts build budgets, incremental budgeting is a highly simplistic model that assumes that the previous level of expenditure is a reasonable base for estimating needs and revenues for the next budget cycle."[22] This very basic process merely adds increments to the various parts of the last budget to produce the next budget. Although its lack of complexity has merit, and the process itself has some logic and has received a great deal of use over the history of budgeting, incremental budgeting pays little attention to changes or trends in revenue or expenditure or to how the money in the budget is used.

Probably this type of budgeting finds its greatest use today in drafts of the early stages of the budget development process. For example, a school district wishing to finalize its budget in June may use incremental increases for inflation in the cost of paper for the November draft, with more time and concern devoted to how much paper will be used and how it will be used as the school and budget development years progress. This would be a more effective use of incremental budgeting than increasing next year's entire budget by the cost of living or some such increment.

LINE-ITEM BUDGETING

In this budget type, items or objects of expenditure—personnel, supplies, capital outlay—are the focus of analysis, authorization, and control (see Figure 1.4).[23] Line-item budgeting may be little more than incrementally changing the component parts of the entire budget, thereby making the whole budget the sum of all its line-item parts. This is definitely more specific than incremental budgeting as each line in the budget receives separate consideration with each item being increased or decreased by a specific amount.[24] Line-item budgets, however, do not of themselves offer any indication of how allocation decisions are made.

Line-item budgeting was the most commonly used budget type until the 1960s when schools began moving toward budgeting that was more related to items purchased. Many schools continue with the line-item approach with greater specificity and/or the lumping together of lines into programs and with more

Instructional Supplies	1996–97 Expenditures	1998–99 Projections
Typing paper	$7034	$8123
Tablets	2331	2558
Construction paper	1109	1344
Pencils	6335	6789
Rulers	564	500
	. . .*	
Total inst. supp.	$35,098	$39,934

*This symbol,. . ., will be used throughout to indicate where less significant material is not included.

Figure 1.4 Portion of a sample line-item budget.

desirable evidence of planning rather than just acknowledgement of history. The line-item approach will probably always have its adherents because it has been around for so long, it is understandable, and it provides control. Modifying it to provide more information useful to planning permits the line-item type of budgeting to remain useful to many budgeters.

PROGRAM BUDGETING

Program or function–object budgeting is a more modern, more sophisticated type of budgeting. Plans and appropriations are made on the basis of expected results of the component organizational units.[25] The budget that comes from this is related to the school organization's program structure.

Figure 1.5 is a very much simplified example. Today's budgets of any type would generally also include explanatory text, and a program budget would very likely include more cross summaries. For example, in addition to the summary of

Program	1996–97 Budget	Actual 1996–97 Expenditure	1997–98 Budget
High school reading			
Salaries	$41,000	40,600	41,400
Supplies and paper	300	455	510
	. . .		
West elem. reading			
Salaries	15,000	14,900	15,200
Supplies and paper	400	580	635
	. . .		
Total reading	$307,450	305,894	318,100
	. . .		

Figure 1.5 Portion of a sample program budget.

the reading program in the district, a program budget would include summaries of each building, salaries, supplies, and paper.

Through computer technology, program budgeting permits the analysis of cost by component, which, in turn, permits cost-effectiveness comparisons (see Budget Example, pp. 107–108, 110–113). Applying an earlier example, paper is not just all lumped together in one line item but is in each program utilizing paper: the English department, an elementary school, third grade, or the dropout prevention program. Per-pupil costs can be easily examined by program.

Program budgeting permits the following to be addressed: Does the football program really carry the other sports? Do the results of the new reading program justify its cost? What causes school A's operating costs to be so much higher than school B's?

Program budgeting facilitates seeing how school activities and the budget are related and interdependent. Program budgeting "conceptually moves the budget process into a conscious recognition of the relationship between money and programs, and the opportunity now becomes available to think of the budgeting process as an educational enterprise."[26]

Program budgeting lends itself to administrative variation. School building or district administrators can add levels of sophistication to this type of budgeting, which, in turn, permit the levels of planning and accountability they seek. A drawback, however, can arise if it becomes too complicated as administrators and policy makers demand it to do more. Program budgeting can take on a life of its own.

Program, Planning and Budgeting Systems (PPBS) is a logical improvement on earlier program budgeting. It made programs or units within the school organization responsible for their own goals and direction.[27] PPBS is more planning oriented. Each program or unit develops plans that direct it toward its educational goals. This plan improves budgeting by providing a planning component as well as goal orientation. PPBS also contributes to the district's accountability by focusing on results by each program.

"Budgeters are powerful but ignorant; planners are knowledgeable but powerless; what could be more desirable, thought the proponents of PPBS, than combining the virtues of both classes by making budgeters into planners."—Aaron Wildavsky, *Budgeting: A Comparative Theory of Budgetary Process*[28]

With the addition of evaluation to PPBS's planning concentration, Program, Planning, Budgeting, Evaluation Systems (PPBES) brings further improvements to program budgeting. The notion described above, whereby programs within a district can be measured in terms of expected outcomes, is made even more useful. To the example in Figure 1.5 would be added an assessment of the paper cost increase, which may be simply due to an increase in the cost of the paper. If the increase really is for the purpose of funding an improved outcome, that would be described in measurable terms as part of the budget document. Evaluation adds accountability and, as part of program budgeting, leads to more cost effectiveness in the budgeting process.

ZERO-BASED BUDGETING

The name of this type of budgeting is self-defining. Zero-based budgeting is founded on the concept that each budget or budget component starts at zero each new budget period. It is the opposite of incremental budgeting and as such is the darling of the anti-taxes crowd. "ZBB is an example of external political realities pressing change on educational organizations during an era of fiscal austerity and retrenchment in the nation."[29]

Hack, Candoli, and Ray point out that zero-based budgeting "is not simply a derivative of PPBES."[30] They go on to write that ZBB's advantages include improving on PPBES by focusing management processes on analysis and decision making; requiring ongoing, detailed evaluations of operations, efficiency, and cost effectiveness; identifying similar functions among different staff for comparison and evaluation; and providing management training and participation in decision making. They then cite disadvantages including that administration and communication are more complicated, and budget preparation is more time consuming. Also, they note that evaluative data often are not available and evaluation of dissimilar functions is not feasible.[31]

Although it could have some merit when administratively applied to a program on an ad hoc basis, ZBB appears too complicated and negative to be used in toto. The idea of completely justifying every aspect of every budget every year requires a great deal of effort and expense and annual replication. However, for example, a new program could quite sensibly require complete justification, as could new resources for existing programs, thereby exercising caution, efficiency, and accountability, particularly in austere times.[32] Administrators in this decade and the next would probably be better advised to learn from ZBB that justification is a fundamental and mandatory tool of budgeting than to allow themselves to have ZBB mandated by a board of directors annoyed by rising budgets that lack proper justification.

DECENTRALIZED BUDGETING

The now commonly held tenet of school administration, even management in general, that decisions are best made at the lowest possible level has led to budgeting being more decentralized. This is often referred to as site-based budgeting, a concept that has budgeting decisions made at the individual school level, in some cases by site councils, which include parents and other non-educator members of the school community.

According to Hartman,[33] highly centralized budgeting has all important decisions made in the central office. This is evidenced by all students at a grade level tending to be treated the same by the budget, whereas a highly decentralized budgeting process has nearly all decisions made at the local school, thereby creating a budget that treats students differently by school. In decentralized budgeting a lump sum of money is sent to the site for allocation according to a site-developed plan. It would seem that there are many possible degrees of budgeting decentralization between the two extremes and that districts could select the degree of decentralization that is most appropriate, recognizing the readiness of those involved. In fact, Hack, Candoli, and Ray indicate that even "most school districts that have moved to building budgeting have retained centralized and district level budgeting for capital outlay, maintenance, administration, and other funds and accounts that are districtwide rather than individual school building functions."[34]

SUMMARY

The foregoing discussions lead the authors to the following theoretical and experienced-based conclusions and recommendations as bases for budget development.

School district budgeting should be a planning process with a goal orientation. The purposes of budgeting are to provide the schools with a planning process, needs assessment, goals, program and fiscal performance evaluation, justification, an approval process, and control. Planning and goal setting should be based on knowledge of current (and a reasonable prediction of future) environmental conditions in local education. Budget development goals should be measurable, and their costs should be included.

Educational leaders should determinedly use the budgeting process to translate vision and goals into reality. Dependable information about recent fiscal history is essential to budgeting. History, however, is a guide, not necessarily a basis for budgeting.

Budget development must be open, communicative, and involve those affected by the results. Educational leaders should translate their vision into reality through the accomplishment of budgetary goals. Goal setting is a budgetary tool. Budgeting is a leadership tool and should be for improvement, not the status quo.

The budgeting process, of necessity, includes analysis of cost effectiveness. Some form of program budgeting should be utilized, the level of sophistication prompted by the level of planning and program accountability sought. Budget development should be decentralized to the degree possible given district attitudes, philosophy, and readiness.

CHAPTER 2

Planning a Budget Development Process: Practical Considerations

KEEPING BUDGETING POSITIVE

IT does not take hours of scholarly research for a school administrator to learn that the budget development process in our public schools has become increasingly negative. Any educator who reads the evening paper or who leads in budget development realizes taxpayers these days are negatively more than positively affecting budgets and budgeting. These same experienced educators also recognize that school boards have been pushed from their historically positive stances relative to funding education to ones of remarkably negative, even nasty, approaches to budgeting for our children's education.

It appears certain that teachers, principals, and superintendents don't believe negative approaches are as effective as positive ones when it comes to successful budgeting. How, then, do things get turned around?

In the mid-1980s one of the authors wrote in a Pennsylvania school board journal[35] of his experience in preventing negative approaches to budget development by encouraging positive leadership in planning and goal setting. While utilizing participatory decision making, a concept recommended elsewhere in this book, the district established a calendar (see Budget Calendar later, Figure 2.5) that called for setting goals early in the budget process and at all levels of the district.

It must be noted here that throughout the budgeting process, the board of school directors kept its traditional and legally supported role of public decision making at the top of the organizational chart while receiving year-long input from the professional educators through appropriate channels and from all organizational levels and programs. Granted, some budget cutting was still necessary, but it was done according to agreed upon priorities established as part of goal setting and couched in positive terms as a result of direction-providing goals set by the board according to a highly participatory process. Much of the negativism usually associated with budget reduction was avoided by positive goal orientation facilitated by participation and communication.

Additionally, the board directed implementation and budgeting of the district's numerous planning efforts such as the comprehensive, five-year educational plan; the computer education plan; the curriculum cycle; and the long-range maintenance plan. These plans all set positive, progressive tones and greatly eased budgeting, particularly helping to minimize micro-managing by board members.

One point of basic board/administration relations also helped prevent negativism: when reductions in a budget draft were deemed necessary by the board, the administration was always informed of the dollar amount by which the budget was to be reduced, not the items to be removed or the areas of the budget to be reduced. The administration, faculty, and staff who built the budget then recommended reduction according to their best professional judgment.

REVENUE PLANNING

Revenue planning is probably one of the more experientially based forms of planning. A theoretical element, however, can be seen in a point made by Hack, Candoli, and Ray, among others: the revenue plan should be developed concurrently with the expenditure and educational plans. The budgeting process becomes a focal point for all three.[36]

However, given the fact that the fifty states have widely varying systems of state financial support for public education, it is difficult to prescribe a generic method for planning school district revenue sources (federal, state, local) for all districts. In 1990–91, twenty-three states used a foundation program approach to state funding of school districts with mandatory local effort, and in fifteen states local effort was not mandatory. In the same year six states utilized percent-equalization programs, of which five had mandatory local effort, and two states each had full state funding, flat grants from the state, or guaranteed tax base/yield programs.[37] Obviously, this array of methods of state funding causes even more methods of predicting revenue needs at the local district level.

Additionally, the relationships among the three funding sources also varies from district to district. Although the average distribution in 1994–95 was federal revenue 3.1%, state revenue 44.6%, and local revenue 52.3% of district budgets,[38] the relationships varied from district to district according to such factors as wealth, enrollment, federal impact, or local taxing effort. Most school districts rely on the local real estate property tax for the majority of local revenue, but there is still a variety of local taxes and local taxing methods across the nation.

Therefore, here we will simply advocate that districts determine the most workable planning methods for themselves and modify them as experience

Revenue Sources	School Years		
	1994–95	1989–90	1984–85
Local	52.3%	55.9	53.0
State	44.6	41.4	43.4
Federal	3.1	2.7	3.6

Figure 2.1 National average percentages of revenue sources.

dictates. However, see also Revenue Planning in Chapter 3 for some activities in revenue planning during the budgeting process.

REVENUE AND EXPENDITURE COMPARISONS

It should be helpful for budgeters to have some idea of average revenues and expenditures nationally and for an entire state. Figures 2.1–2.4 are provided here for that purpose, but it must be kept in mind that circumstances can readily be visualized that would cause a district to vary from the average, and, therefore, variation does not necessarily indicate either competence or waste. For example, in most states community wealth is a factor in the percentage of revenue a district receives from the state, and geographic location is a factor in the percentage of a district's budget expended for environmental conditioning. Age of buildings would be a factor in the percentage for maintenance and operation. These figures are meant as examples and are hardly absolute standards for evaluation of budgeting.

Further examples of these types of comparisons can be found in Figures 4.1 and 4.2.

Allocation	Percent of Total Expenditure*		
	1994–95	1989–90	1984–85
Instructional services	69.4%	67.8	65.2
Student services	7.2	7.5	7.9
School-site leadership	5.5	5.5	5.8
Cent. off. admin. and board service	4.7	4.7	5.0
Maintenance and operations	7.8	8.5	9.0
Environmental conditioning	2.6	3.0	4.1
Other current expenditures	2.7	3.0	3.0
Avg. per pupil expend..	$5767	4741	3170

*Does not include capital outlay or debt service.

Figure 2.2 National average percentages of total current expenditures allocated for various functional categories.

Instruction 1000	Support Services 2000	Non-instructional Services 3000	Facilities Acquisition 4000
60.3%	30.3	2.0	.2

Other Financial uses 5000	Total Expenditure
7.3	100.1

Current Expenditure*	Actual Instructional Expenditures**
92.6	73.1

*1000, 2000, 3000.
**Instructional expenditures from all categories.

Figure 2.3 Average percentages of budget allocation by function in Pennsylvania Public School Districts, area vocational technical schools, and special schools, 1993–94.

Pupil Personnel 2100	Instructional Staff 2200	Administration 2300	Pupil Health 2400
2.9%	2.7	6.7	1.0

Business 2500	Operations and Maintenance 2600	Student Transportation 2700	Central 2800
1.3	10.0	4.9	.6

Other Support 2900	Total Support Services 2000
.2	30.3

Figure 2.4 Average percentages of budget for support services expenditures in pennsylvania school districts, area vocational technical schools, and special schools, 1993–94.

PARTICIPATION IN BUDGET DEVELOPMENT

As pointed out several places in Chapter 1, budgeting should no longer be done just by one or two administrators in each district. Rather, the people affected by its results must have some role in the process, varying from district to district and depending on the type of budgeting utilized. Obviously, a decentralized process of program budgeting in an open, communicative district will have nearly all personnel and much of the school community involved (also see Communications, this chapter). But who should be involved and to what degree?

Experience seems to reveal several arguments for involving all faculty and staff to the degree that they can contribute to the process. It is no longer argued that teachers are not the best judge of teaching materials. They are, just as maintenance personnel are the best judges of maintenance supplies, materials, and equipment.

Twenty years ago, an early exercise of participatory decision making permitted the custodians in one district to graphically show that the cheapest floor cleaner and wax were, in fact, the most expensive approach to floor care because they had to be used more than twice as often to achieve the desired result. At the suggestion of the custodial staff, the district budgeted for the more expensive floor cleaner and wax and then budgeted for a reduction in the previously projected increase in staffing. The net saving was substantial—people cost more than floor-care products.

If a budget development process communicates well in all directions, morale is better because with increased participation in budget development people know they've been heard, and they know they are helping to improve how they do their jobs. The communications organization must be in place in order that faculty, staff, and others involved know what decisions were made above them and why. All staff have to be told why their proposals didn't make it into the final budget.

In a rural district the educational technology and vocational agriculture faculties along with the district's maintenance staff proposed that the budget being developed include a 50% increase for lumber in one year. In addition to the finished lumber normally purchased annually from a national supplier, the teachers and staff members proposed purchasing, storing, curing, and then finishing raw lumber from area saw mills for use the following year at 50% of the annual cost. The budgeted amount for successive years, then, was half what was budgeted in the past. It should be noted that, although the proposal provided students increased instructional opportunities, it also generated more work for the faculty and staff members who proposed it, a fact they were well aware of when they proposed it.

Teachers generally are interested in increasing learning opportunities for their students, but they also are interested in best utilizing the available instructional dollars. Historically, their involvement in budget development has done both.

In increasing faculty/staff/citizen involvement in the budget process, the administration has to recognize the logistical problems involved and establish organizational and communicative steps that facilitate successful participation by people whose jobs are not customarily administration. For example, parents should be involved in the early goal-setting and needs-assessing stages of budgeting rather than later nuts-and-bolts stages. Business men and women from the community can be involved in evaluating your budget process or reviewing budget proposals that touch on their realms of expertise.

Teachers should have input in the process by department, grade level, or school and can be of great value in the initial stages of budgeting, but they also should be given the opportunity to determine what comes out of the budget when money must be removed. Note that the board should say how much money is included in the budget, rarely which items.

In the days before participatory budgeting was commonplace, one of the authors, in his first full year as superintendent, found himself in August with a budget adopted by the board in June that included $200,000 more in state subsidy than the legislature ultimately and belatedly provided. In a move that permanently instilled in him a high level of confidence in teachers' willingness and ability to help in times of crisis as well as during peace and prosperity, the superintendent made the detailed portions of the budget applicable to each school available to each faculty and asked for their ideas on what expenditure items should be reconsidered. The same was asked of the support staff.

The results argued strongly for more participation in budget development. Faculty and staff demonstrated admirable priorities and intestinal fortitude. Most responses offered viable, sensible reasons for cuts suggested. Although most ideas were proposed just for the immediate crisis, some provided opinions like, "We don't know why this is funded now or ever." One such program, while only costing about $6000 per year, was cited by every elementary faculty as educationally unsound. After 20 unpopular years the program was discontinued.

The next budget cycle in that district involved the faculty and staff from the beginning. The most Neanderthalian administrator and the most cynical teacher became believers.

THE BUDGET CALENDAR

An annual calendar of the school entity's budget process is essential for organization, standardization, and communication, in addition to other typical calendar purposes. Figure 2.5 is only for illustration, although it has been used successfully by a district for a number of years. A budget calendar should serve the particular school entity's needs. Time lines, obviously, will differ from place to place or between types of schools as would activities and their order.

The example here afforded the district the organization and standardization they wanted and eased communication of the process. Annual, wide-spread publication made the process clear to budgeters and community members alike. Its publication also advertised time lines, format, and emphasis. Every interested member of the school community knew how and when district goals and priorities were established. Budgeters could hardly be accused of secrecy.

EVALUATION OF EDUCATIONAL QUALITY AND EFFECTIVENESS

The story exists of the wife of a very successful and mobile executive who, after moving to one of suburban Philadelphia's "lighthouse" school districts, remarked that her children now would have attended school in twelve of the country's ten best districts.

Much has been written about educational quality, what it is, and how to achieve it. A quality education has become part of the American dream and, therefore, part of political and educational rhetoric. It also should be part of any writing on educational budgeting.

Quality in education, however, is hard to pin down, particularly relative to cost, and, in fact, may be more reputed than reality. School reputation tends to be derived from community wealth and things like the number of Merit finalists. The former is only a good indicator, if appropriately used, and the latter is barely more than an indicator of where parents of intelligent children choose to live, perhaps only an addition to an undeserved reputation.

It would seem today that effectiveness would be a good measure of educational quality. How effective is the reading program or facility maintenance? How successful are the school's graduates? Do all students have all the opportunities they should have? How effective are the district's goals in improving what the schools do, and how well are they met?

In a period as concerned with accountability as the one in which we live, measuring effectiveness ought to be a normal part of the budget process. Most schools have some form of program evaluation. Most districts have

Goals established	The board of school directors establishes broad, long-range, annually-reviewed goals that address the district's mission statement.	August
Goals specified and aimed toward budget development	Faculty, through grade levels, curriculum committees and departments, develop specific, measurable goals or objectives within the board goals.	September-October
Goals tentatively adopted	Board of school directors tentatively adopts goals to serve as backdrop and guidelines for budget development.	January
Priorities set for faculty/ staff budgeting and requests developed	The administration sets and communicates to faculty priorities and guidelines for initial development of budgetary requests. Faculty and staff develop budgetary requests for submission to district office. Priorities will require analysis of need for and success of existing program components in order to best use limited resources.	December-January
Initial drafts of budget presented	The administration reports, in summary fashion, the first drafts of the budget to the board at public meetings. Board members comment, question, provide direction, and gain understanding, but no formal action is taken.	February-April
Tentative adoption of budget	Through work sessions and regular public meetings, the board of school directors will have discussed proposals for and drafts of the various budget sections. The administration will have adjusted the proposed budget to reflect these board discussions and will propose a final draft for tentative adoption. Although individual members or the entire board may react positively or negatively to programs or other items in the proposed budget and because this is an interactive process, it shall be the administration's task to recommend what is needed to meet the goals and address the mission in consultation with faculty leaders.	May
Final adoption	After considering any recommendations from the administration, the board will adopt the budget.	June

Figure 2.5 Budget development calendar.

personnel evaluation systems and methodologies for evaluating the effectiveness of supplies, materials, and equipment they use. If they don't, they certainly should. It is also necessary to have evaluation built into the budgeting process.

McGee and Fountain, in the article "Linking Performance Measures and Budgets,"[43] adapted for school districts a model from the state of Texas for developing the links among planning, performance measures, and budgeting. Figure 2.6 graphically points up one way evaluation can serve as a connection between planning in terms of mission and goals and line items in the budget, whether the budgeting is centralized or decentralized and regardless of how program centered. Figure 2.7 portrays a mission statement. Refer to Chapter 1, p. 8 for examples of goals and objectives/activities (strategies). Also see Budget Example, pp. 88, 90–92, 134–135.

The governing board, faculty, staff, and citizens would find a district's written mission statement useful in understanding a school program. The district could graphically show expected results in proposing a new program and evaluative results in justifying existing programs.

The budget process should include evaluation as justification for items and programs included in the budget. At the same time, it should present how programs that the district is funding lead to the successful meeting of goals toward the district's mission. Evaluation as part of budgeting ought to demonstrate school effectiveness and quality. See Budget Example, pp. 82, 118–119.

"Administrators must always finally recognize the real purpose of the schools is to make a difference in student outcomes—a difference that will have to be achieved in a different milieu than has historically been the reality."—Thompson, Wood, and Honeyman, *Fiscal Leadership for Schools*[44]

COMMUNICATIONS IN BUDGETING

Probably the most notable change in school district budgeting in the last few decades is the interest in and reliance upon communications in the process. No longer does the superintendent sit down in May with his/her secretary and put together an unquestioned and uncommunicated budget. Now school boards require budgeters to seek input from all aspects of the school community and to routinely provide information throughout budgeting, including after the budget's adoption. Just as budget development is planning, it is also communication.

Strategic Planning	*Performance Measures*	*Budget*
Mission A statement of what the district does, why it does it, for whom it does it—its reason for existence.		
Philosophy The expression of the core values and operating principals for the conduct of the agency in achieving its mission.		
Internal/External Assessment An evaluation of the key factors that influence the success of the district in achieving its mission.		
District Goals The general ends toward which programs direct their efforts.		
Objectives → Clear targets for specific action that quantify progress toward meeting a particular goal.	**Outcome Measures** Quantifiable results measuring how pupils and/or the public are benefited by meeting program objectives.	
Strategies Methods by which a program seeks to accomplish its goals and objectives.	**Output Measures** → Quantity of program workload and work product as it pursues its strategies.	**Line Items** Items of appropriation in the budget.
	· **Efficiency measures** Program workload unit costs or time for completion.	
	· **Explanatory/Input Measures** External factors relating to program operations.	

Figure 2.6 Linking planning, performance measures, and the budget.

OUR OVERALL MISSION IS TO LEAD OUR COMMUNITY IN DEVELOPING THE FULL POTENTIAL OF EACH OF OUR STUDENT'S INTELLECTUAL, ETHICAL, PHYSICAL, CREATIVE, CULTURAL, SOCIAL, AND TECHNOLOGICAL CAPABILITIES TO MEET OUR SOCIETY'S EVER-CHANGING NEEDS, RECOGNIZING OUR COMMUNITY'S RESOURCES.

To accomplish this mission we commit ourselves, our energies, and our resources to the following:

- We will endeavor to keep every student in school, with minimal absences from tasks, until graduation.
- The best available faculty and staff will be employed and developed to provide quality instruction, counseling, and other support.
- We will provide unique as well as traditional experiences for our students, experiences to broaden understanding and reinforce learning.
- All school service functions will be to facilitate instruction, and all school activities will be carried out in a safe and orderly learning environment.
- Areas of affective concentration across the K–12 program will include ethics, responsibility, and service.
- Instruction will be as individualized as feasible.
- Home/school communication as well as parenting education will be stressed.

Figure 2.7 Mission statement.

"Communications and public relations aspects of the budget are important. Information needs to be provided in terms that are concrete, not the abstract totals. Most individuals will never earn in a lifetime what most districts spend in a single year. As such, explanation of an expenditure with, 'its only $100,000,' is not within the individual frame of reference. What the public does understand is the cost per pupil or the average teacher salary."
—PSBA, *Understanding School Finance*[45]

In a 1993 study, school business officials identified nineteen critical success factors (CSF) for school business administrators. Ranking third and fourth were oral communications skills and written communications skills with 91.3% and 90.8% of participants rating them very or extremely important.[46]

"The public schools belong to the public. For years little has been done to help administrators communicate effectively with the community, staff, and students. With taxes continuing to go up, taxpayers are demanding to know what the schools are doing with their money. Administrators face crisis after crisis—many of them easily traced to poor communication somewhere along the line. These crises are eroding the once solid confidence the public had in public education. Too many administrators have attempted to hide problems, hoping they would disappear before the public discovered them. This approach might have worked in the days when people believed that school officials possessed a special sort of omniscience. It isn't working today. It won't work tomorrow. Citizens, feeling they are shareholders in the schools, are seeking a piece of the action. They have entrusted their two most prized possessions—their children and their money—to school officials, and they want to know what's being done with them. The administrator who does not think of communication when he/she considers accountability, bond issues, student riots, teacher demands, complaints at board meetings, and community group pressures isn't prepared for today's challenges."—Hack, Candoli, and Ray[47]

In a chapter on management application, Hack, Candoli, and Ray cite the following principles of communication.

> Communication has to be honest, thorough, and valid. An innovation should not be announced with fanfare and glowing generalities in September and completely ignored after a spring evaluation indicates the need for either a major overhaul of the program or its abandonment.
>
> Good communication should be a two-way system. Not only do school officials inform, but they are kept informed. Not only do they state opinions and express needs, but they listen to opinions and desires of others.
>
> The communication system is for all people. The audience is not just teachers, not just parents, not just community leaders. The audience is everybody, including students.
>
> The communications system is continuous. The good school communications system does not operate only before tax levies, only in quarterly newsletters, only when the news media will print articles about the system. District officials should be consciously operating their two-way communication system every day, even though the same things do not necessarily happen every day.
>
> A good communication system is not system-oriented. A proper system includes site-based communication.[48]

In this same chapter Hack et al. describe eighteen suggestions for obtaining feedback.[49] Several ideas that are more practical for budgeting are establishing advisory committees, listening to what is said at meetings of service groups, including questionnaires in newsletters, noting questions asked by reporters at news conferences and after board meetings, and being candid with municipal officials and civic leaders.

Similarly practical for the budgeting process are suggested communications enhancers offered by Gary Campbell, who begins by stating, "Listening to your constituents is much more important than any strategy you might devise to tell them things."[50] Some of Campbell's communication tips are

- Know your audience and tailor information to their interests.
- Through personal contact and community visibility, communicate on an understandable level.
- Build relationships that provide faith in your budget and community trust in school people.
- Give the community the personalized information they want.
- Don't just complain and don't always complain.
- Thank people for support.
- Make all communications interesting, positive, and simple.
- Keep staff informed.
- Don't promise what you can't or won't deliver.
- Promote your stewardship image.
- Relate budget information to instructional output.[51]

In their *School Administrator's Budget Handbook*, Ridler and Shockley point out the need for budgeters to know the community's educational priorities through vehicles such as reading the news articles; meetings with business and industry leaders, service clubs, and PTAs; and informal questionnaires.[52] Ridler and Shockley go on to say,

> There are numerous groups and individuals who realize that the quality of the district's schools affects the quality of life in the entire community. These citizens believe that quality schools:
>
> - present a better educational program for their children, and the children will be more successful when they graduate.
> - help attract business and industry to the community along with a stronger tax base.
> - help to keep real estate values high.
> - present a greater variety of programs for all of the citizens, including both children and adults.[53]

It is the job of budget developers "to work with these various groups in the school district, provide up-to-date and correct information concerning existing and needed programs, create opportunities for discussion, and make certain that the groups understand that you value their input."[54] Two more communicative devices suggested by Ridler and Shockley are less commonly cited but no less suggestive of pervasive communications: keep staff and student leaders apprised of the status of appropriate budget sections and keep appropriate parts of the community, and the community in general, apprised of the whens and whys of school group fundraising activities.[55]

In summary, good, two-way communications is a necessary budgetary task and should pervade the budgetary process and the school community. Successful budgeters communicate well. See Budget Example, particularly pp. 79–104.

MULTI-YEAR BUDGETS

Because inaccuracies increase in budgeting for more than one year there is a natural aversion to preparing longer-period budgets, but there are good reasons for developing them. Communication and preparation are the two most obvious. The board, the administration, and the school community need to know that the budget for two years from now will increase substantially because the high school building project's debt service will begin. See Budget Example, pp. 115–118, 122–123, 131–133. By the same token, the board, administration, and community should be aware that in 1998–99 school taxes from the new industrial park on the edge of town will begin to accrue to the district. Obviously, accuracy becomes more of a challenge the further budgeters look into the future, but multi-year budgets are useful and not difficult to develop as part of the annual budget development process (see Figure 3.3). Long-range planning is now such an integral part of school budgeting that a multi-year budget should assist in its funding as well as communicating how the long-range plan will affect future budgets.

"In order for a plan or forecast to be an effective tool, it must be linked inextricably to the budget development process. Financial planning and budgeting should be considered as one concept with two elements."—Michael A. Jacoby, "The Future Demands It Now—Multi-Year Budgeting"[56]

In describing a multi-year budget model in an Illinois school district, Jacoby[57] notes that five expenditure categories should be forecast in the multi-year budget: current program, enrollment impact, program improvement, large projects, and contingency. Figure 3.3, p. 42, is an example of multi-year budgeting used by a Pennsylvania school district; it contains forecasting in Jacoby's categories.

Multi-year budgeting is also used in curriculum cycles and long-range maintenance plans with the above-cited benefits and drawbacks (see Chapter 3).

CONTRACTING FOR SERVICES AND PRIVATIZATION

Decision making about contracting for services and other forms of privatization are not in and of themselves part of the budgetary process, nor should they be. This section admonishes budgeters against the common mistake of only seeing the potential savings in turning some aspect of the district's operation over to a private organization. This may be a good idea for study, but it is dangerously short sighted to engage in the contracting of services without thorough exploration prior to any relative budget decisions.

The board and administration of a suburban school district believed their costs of custodial care in the district's buildings were exorbitant. They felt their custodial staff was so well paid because of employee seniority and long-term employer generosity at the collective bargaining table that it would be easy to get a private firm to clean the schools much more cheaply. They were correct. They also were correct in getting and following legal advice on how to contract for services without running afoul of labor law. They were not correct in ignoring other factors in turning a major support service over to non-employees of the district.

A city firm was contracted to clean one building, the middle school, on a trial basis, and unquestionably money began to be saved. However, the people doing the cleaning had no commitment to the school district and in many cases were hired on a day-to-day basis by the contractor. Certainly little screening was done. Within weeks enough equipment and supplies had been stolen, particularly on the night shifts, to prompt the district to return to employing their own custodians. It does not take the loss of many televisions, VCRs, microscopes, band instruments, or much cafeteria food for the savings to be offset.

Schools have privatized maintenance and transportation for years, but now contracting is for larger portions of the district budget, and legal and performance issues are becoming apparent concerns. Here are some guidelines: Know your subcontractor, set performance standards, familiarize yourself with all of the terms of the contract before signing, have contract reviewed for any group where there is a potential for conflict, make a full disclosure to your staff, have an open hearing on the subject for the public, evaluate your current staff well, be prepared for notoriety, and review your relationship with your current vendors.[58]

Privatization of everything, from what has been traditionally contracted out, such as transportation to instruction, which is still in the exploratory stages of privatization, is very much a consideration of today's schools. Because of the strong interest today in making schools more businesslike, there are specific questions that should be asked. Several of these questions Russo and Harris address in an article cautionarily entitled "Buyer Beware":

- Public education should not jump at privatization as a simple solution to a multifaceted problem.
- Appropriate, effective evaluation of moves to privatization must occur.
- Education's stakeholders must be empowered to realize what is being purchased for them.
- Impacts of privatization, including potential labor strife and other hidden costs, have to be examined on a cost–benefit basis.[59]

All of the issues of contracting out school services have to be studied by a district considering privatization. Of at least equal importance, the study should be accomplished prior to budget decisions related to privatization being made, not during or, worse yet, after.

FUND BALANCE

The fund balance may seem to be a very specific part of budgeting to be considered here, but the management of the fund balance is causing serious but preventable problems in many school districts. These problems are often of simultaneous conflict between the board and its educators and the board and its community (see box). Fund balance is the term for district reserves of money accumulated since the district's inception by surpluses at the end of the budget year.[60] It is the accumulation of funds resulting from the district raising more revenue than it expends in any one year. Based on that definition, the causes of the conflicts mentioned above are not obvious.

There exists in rural Pennsylvania a tiny school district that for years had a large fund balance. In fact, because of this relatively large reserve the board viewed itself as wise and prudent, serious guardians of the taxpayers' dollars. It goes without saying that this wise and prudent board did not raise taxes for years.

Along came a period of several years in the 1980s with large increases in costs, particularly for salaries. The board, still viewing themselves as wise and prudent, and continuing to be proud of their tradition of no tax increase, used the fund balance to prevent any increase in taxes. In 3 years the fund balance was zero.

The board then was forced to double taxes in one year and raise them another 30% the next year. The sages on the board were voted out of office when their terms were up, and every superintendent in the state used this district, or one making a similar error, as a horrible example to terrify his or her board into careful use of the fund balance.

Look at Figure 2.8 for an example similar to what administrators have been showing boards ever since there have been administrators and boards who differ over the use of fund balances.

The district in Figure 2.8 began 1994–95 with a fund balance of $1 million, a sensible reserve of 5% of its $20,000,000 budget for that year. The increase in fund balance by $100,000 (1.5%) to $1,100,000 during 1994–95 is not unreasonable or unexpected. Increases in expenditures of $400,000 during 1995–96 resulted in the need to utilize reserves. That is the reason for having reserves and is not of itself a problem. The fund balance is now at $800,000, also not yet a problem. Note that revenue has not increased nor is it increased in the next two

	1994–95	1995–96	1996–97	1997–98	1998–99
7/1 Fund Balance	$1,000,000	1,100,000	800,000	100,000	−1,000,000
Revenue	20,000,000	20,000,000	20,000,000	20,000,000	21,500,000
Expend.	19,900,000	20,300,000	20,700,000	21,100,000	21,500,000
6/30 Fund Balance	1,100,000	800,000	100,000	−1,000,000	

Figure 2.8 Fund balance problems.

years, but expenditures have increased during this period. In fact, from 1994–95 until 1997–98 expenditures have not been totally funded by the budget. They have increased by a modest rate but can no longer be funded by reserves, which are now depleted. Revenue must now be increased and it must be increased by 12.5% to pay off the $1,000,000, probably borrowed to avoid a deficit at the end of 1997–98, and the routine increase to be expected in expenditures for 1998–99. School administrators can use Figure 2.8 to show boards how easily and quickly a seemingly comfortable reserve can turn into a deficit that warrants a huge tax increase. The readily seen cause of this problem is the steady increase in expenditures not funded by the budgeted revenue. This is cumulative and ultimately will dictate funding in the annual budget.

The nature of school budgets—that is, annual revenue generally and necessarily exceeding annual expenditure—will cause a positive balance at the end of most years. Needs for a reasonable fund balance include the following: uncertainty of state funds, self-insurance, contingencies, and periodic large expenditure.[61] Allen offers the following commonly accepted advice on fund balance. Less than 5% of that year's budget is cause for concern but a fund balance of more than 10% could be seen as excessive.[62] Budgeters in individual districts may have good reasons to vary from these guidelines. The only way to reduce the fund balance by using it as revenue in the budget is to fund non-reoccurring expenditures. Capital expenditures paid for with fund balance money do not cause the problem shown in Figure 2.8, operational supplies or salaries do.

RISK TAKING

One of the more controversial and, when applied to budgeting, often questionable elements of leadership is the taking of risks. More than likely all leaders engage in it to one degree or another and from time to time, but rarely is taking risks without consequences, and, in the public school budget development process, ethics can be called into question.

"Never play with scared money."—Poker maxim

In putting a budget together some risks must be assumed, for budgeting is planning and carries few guarantees. However, budgeting risks must be justifiable, they must be prudent, and the chances for success or benefit should outweigh the penalties for failure.

A Common Budgeting Risk Benefit/Penalty Scenario

You are superintendent of a school district that normally receives 30% of its annual revenue in the form of state subsidy. By state law, your board and the state legislature are required to adopt their respective annual budgets by June 30. It is June 1 and the legislature, not known to slavishly adhere to its own regulations, is not close to passing its budget. Consequently, you do not know what to budget for revenue from state subsidy. Your board is not inclined to see this as a state-created problem requiring them to be understanding of your dilemma. No, they view this as another reason you are paid a salary rivaling Michael Jordan's, and they expect you to recommend a balanced budget to them according to their normal calender. (The latter really is your job.)

You, no stranger to problems created by others but requiring to be dealt with successfully by you, know the legislature will more than likely stumble into adopting a budget in July without apology to you. You also believe your salary should be closer to Michael's. Toward that end, after consulting with your state representative and others knowledgeable of what you can expect when the legislature finally acts, you recommend a balanced budget that contains your best-educated, but not necessarily most optimistic, estimate of state subsidy.

In addition, you propose to your board a prioritized list of offsets for any shortfalls the state budget may deal you. These will be, for the most part, delayed purchases, new programs or program expansions put on hold, or the tapping of reserves. This all must be done with the confidence (see box above) born of your diligent homework and common sense.

If your confidence is justified, the legislature will grant a subsidy that is more than you planned, and you can recommend to the board how the additional money will be used and plan a response to questions about why, on your Jordan-like salary, you couldn't come closer in your budgeting.

Although some administrators occasionally may adopt the mushroom farmer approach to dealing with the board (keep in the dark and cover with horse manure), risk taking is a time for candor. The board, or superior in the case of subordinate administrators, should be apprised of the risks proposed in order that it/he/she has the opportunity to reject the approach. Rejection does not let the administrator off the hook but, rather, dictates that he/she make alternative proposals until one is acceptable.

Risk taking should be a weighing of cost versus benefits, an analysis of potential penalties compared to potential gains. Some administrators go so far as to graphically juxtapose the comparisons and even attempt to assign numerical values to the factors comprising the two sides of the issue. The latter is easier in instances related to budgeting than might be expected in other cases. Whatever the administrative methodology, budgeting leadership requires prudent rather than daredevil approaches to the taking of risks and an analysis of all potential options for handling the risk outcomes.

Another Common Budgeting Risk Benefit/Penalty Scenario

You are an elementary principal desiring to initiate a student writing program in your school which addresses a district goal of measurably improved student writing. Your role in the relatively decentralized budget development process is to propose and justify expenditures totaling $850,000 for your site/school. Although your superintendent favors the proposed program and expects you to budget for it, she also has authority to approve or reject your proposals for funding it. The program would cost approximately $50,000 per year, most of it for supplies, materials, and two part-time staff. You see four funding prospects:

(1) Propose that, since the writing initiative is a current and popular academic goal, the meeting of which has permanent benefit to students, you increase taxes one-quarter mill, earmarked for the project.
You reject this idea because the project would be initiated in only one of four elementary schools. In addition, you know how superintendents hate to raise taxes even one-quarter mill.

(2) You are writing a grant proposal for funding of this writing project. If awarded to you, the grant would pay for 50% of the cost for 3 years after which time, you could argue, a successful writing project should be locally funded. The smart money is giving you a 50/50 chance of receiving the grant. You hold on to this idea.

(3) The long-range maintenance plan calls for $50,000 in roofing work to be done on your school next year. You, ever the knowledgeable administrator, have heard through your grapevine that the district's roofing consultant now recommends putting off this project for 1 or 2 years.
You reject this idea as not utilizing hard money revenue. Even you don't have the nerve to propose a smoke and mirrors funding—too risky to your credibility.

(4) Three of your senior faculty are expected to retire at the end of the current school year. The district's hiring history tells you that their replacements would probably cost about $51,000 less than next year's salaries of the

projected retirees if they were to stay. The risks with this are two fold. First, only two of the three have submitted letters of retirement, and, second, you could spend more than the historical average in hiring the replacements (but you could also spend less). You decide to go with this fourth option, with the grant idea as a backup in the event that the as yet uncommitted teacher does not retire, and/or the replacements don't save you as much as expected. You have little financial risk, albeit more than with the first option, but this funding notion is apt to be more appealing to your superintendent.

SUMMARY

This chapter and Chapter 1, as well as experience, lead the authors to the following conclusions and recommendations for budgeting.

Administrators should pro-actively assist the board, faculty, and staff in developing a budget from a positive, goal-oriented approach, one that minimizes opportunities for micro-management, cynicism, or dealing in personalities. Budget development should be participatory to the extent that participation is helpful and effective, and roles and expectations must be clear.

The budget development process should include development and circulation of a budget calendar. Budget development has some room for comparing budget categories with those in other districts and recognizing the reasons for comparative differences. Necessary accountability, justification, and support for the budget require evaluation to communicate district quality and effectiveness. Communication must pervade the entire budgeting process throughout the school community.

Any privatization of school district services is risky and must be studied in advance of a decision as to hard and soft costs compared to expected benefits.

Maintaining a reasonable fund balance is important. Reducing it when necessary can and must be done without causing future problems.

Budgeting routinely involves taking risks. Risks should always be analyzed for the benefits relative to the penalties possible if anticipated outcomes are not achieved.

CHAPTER 3

Developing the School Budget

SCHOOL budgeting has undergone a metamorphosis during the past two decades. The process had been predicated in the 1960s and 1970s on a line-item or a fund-object basis, whereby budgets and expenditures were delineated by the fiscal resources expended, i.e., instructional salaries, supplies, etc. The movement, however, to performance or program budgeting, wherein the specific purpose or programs associated with organizational goals and desired outcomes are emphasized, has risen to the forefront, thus transferring the focus from inputs to the outputs or results of the organization.

The prime importance or utility of program or goal-oriented budgeting may not lie, then, in obtaining the minimum financial cost to meet the specified goal but, rather, in allowing for rational alternatives or emphasizing various educational objectives. It must be remembered, moreover, that program budgeting is not a substitute for effective administration, nor is it a remedy for organizations that do not have sufficient resources to achieve their objectives.

MISSIONS, VISIONS, AND GOALS

The process of building the school budget effectively begins with formulation of a mission statement and visions for the total educational organization, as well as the development of annual written goals to enable the attainment of the visions.

For the purpose of this book, we define the goals as synonymous with objectives declared annually by the various programs, departments, or levels of the institution.

A CHANGING MISSION?

A school system is designed to bring to each generation of children an awareness of the past, skills they need in the present, and a sense of the challenges and opportunities of the future. This universal mission has been translated over the years with shifting emphases resulting from political, social, and economic forces.

"Within the next decades education will change more than it has changed since the modern school was created by the printed book over three hundred years ago."—Peter Drucker, *The New Realities*[63]

Today, educators face a society with diverse views on the role and content of education. Frequently it is difficult to discern common agreement on the continuing mission in the midst of conflict over the specifics of how to help our children achieve essential skills and knowledge and how to finance the costs of basic education programs. Schools, in general, are now grappling with diminishing financial resources. This factor, in turn, reduces somewhat our capacity to respond to the changing needs of students.

"But the stinging criticisms and widespread unrest that began in the early 1980s have generally been oriented by a distinctive, more narrowly focused theme: that the academic quality of the public schools is unacceptably low. The universal demand, at all levels of government is for reforms that promote academic excellence."—Chubb and Moe, *Politics, Markets and American Schools*[64]

The school community is now experiencing assaults from different but often united segments of the population. Fiscal conservatives, the religious far right, and senior citizens in many parts of the country are actually, and sometimes jointly, moving to limit taxes for schools, often by trying to eliminate school programs that they believe are offensive or not essential. Frequently these folks have clear goals that are counter to or least clearer than those of the public schools.

Perhaps more than ever before, school leaders must clearly define the mission, visions, and goals that will most effectively assist our students. We recognize both that our children need the best education we can offer and that there are very real limitations on our resources. To this end a general set of goals and objectives is described as that proposed from personnel within the school-community environment. Action plans and timetables, known as standards of performance, congruent with these goals are developed at building, grade, and program levels (see Figure 3.1).

Objective: Expand the tech prep program to include applied communications.

Standard of Performance

1. Provide materials and training sessions for staff by August 1.
2. Develop a brochure to facilitate the career pathway concept.
3. Schedule discussion sessions with all tech prep teachers on four occasions during the year.
4. Evaluate the effectiveness of the course through a year-end formal assessment.

Objective: Monitor the implementation and effectiveness of electronic portfolios at Jackson Elementary School.

Standard of Performance

1. Provide a scanner for the portfolio process by August 15.
2. Meet periodically with the Jackson Elementary staff to assess the program's effectiveness.
3. Formulate a year-end recommendation to expand the program across the district or to curtail its use.

Figure 3.1 Action plan.

Goals are by no means exhaustive but are written as a means of focusing efforts. This focus is integral to creating a positive climate for education where excellence is sought, encouraged, and recognized inside and outside the classroom; moreover, this environment is indicative of people working together cooperatively and openly to support each other's efforts on behalf of the children.

GOALS REFLECT VISIONS

These goal statements are divided into categories that reflect a district's visions. While two-way communication obviously is subsumed in all goal statements, there is a need to place further emphasis on the manner in which ideas are expressed and suggestions, criticism, or information offered. Perhaps this factor, more than any other, will determine success in accomplishing the goals and achieving the mission (see Figure 3.2).

IMPORTANCE OF COMMUNICATIONS

Two-way or open communications is an absolute must during the entire budget process—whether that be between the board of education and the superintendent, the superintendent and the business manager, the principal and

VISION: A school-community environment characterized by high expectations, respect for academic excellence, and mutual caring, which motivates students at all grade levels.

Objective: Restructure programs, wherever feasible, for efficiency and effectiveness.

Standard of Performance

1. Continue preparation for block or intensive schedule implementation at the high school.
2. Implement the newly formulated middle school schedule to include the star/homeroom concept and a period 8 enrichment/accelerated program.
3. Explore through a pilot program the introduction of a developmental reading program at the middle school level.

Objective: Establish performance-based student goals so that graduates can apply what they have learned.

Standard of Performance

1. Continue revision of all course guides to reflect an emphasis on performance evaluation.
2. Expand the tech prep curriculum program to include the area of applied communications.
3. Develop indicators of learning for each grade at the elementary school level.

Figure 3.2 Superintendent of schools.

the teachers, etc. This open dialogue is also critical in the formulation of goals and the assessment of progress, or the lack thereof, in the achievement of the written goal statements.

We are all familiar with the principal who submitted to the central office at the beginning of the year goals for his building and then was criticized during the evaluation conference for developing meaningless goals or for pursuing goals that were not in concert with the district's vision. The principal, of course, is not at fault in this instance; district administrators did not communicate their perceptions for implementing the goal activities prior to the ordering of supplies/equipment or staffing.

Building administrators, in turn, who do not communicate to staff whether budget requests are "approved" or "cut" and the rationale for the action undermine the budget process and cause undue frustration and anger on the part of the teaching staff.

LONG-RANGE PLANNING

Financial planning, which follows the development of the mission statement, vision, and goals, usually emanates from a school district's strategic plan or long-range plan (LRP), and in its most comprehensive form it is a multi-year process (see Budget Example, pp. 89, 133–134). Various school organizations in the past have attempted to provide a 5-year budget plan only to discover that the dynamic factors of budgeting make it impossible to realistically plan for more than 2 or 3 years in the future.

The long-range plan, which focused on inputs rather than results, frequently gathered dust on the shelves of the central office. In addition, the LRP was a "top-down" document that had little relationship to the needs of the students and the comprehensive school community. A close examination of the LRP usually revealed textbook statements with little usefulness to the personnel implementing the instructional program.

The strategic plan—a comprehensive process that includes community members, students, staff, and the board of education—has legitimately replaced the antiquated long-range plan. It is a dynamic and ever-changing document that relates directly to the mission, visions, and goals of an organization and directs the programs and activities included in the annual budget.

LONG-RANGE BUDGETS

Often as a device to assist boards and communities in recognizing that budgets will fluctuate from year to year (Figure 3.3), administrators prepare short-term budgets (commonly 2 or 3 years, rarely more than 5) that show predictable fluctuations such as a building project being paid off. As indicated in Chapter 2, these multi-year budgets are only guides and are certainly not used by all school districts, but they frequently provide planning and communications assistance to school leaders who use them.

Note that in Figure 3.3 major changes resulting from predictable increases in salaries, computer purchases, and long-range maintenance expenses as well as revenue increases resulting from the increasing value of a mill of real estate tax permit reasonably accurate projections of millage but also permit a leveling of the millage somewhat.

SCHEDULING ACTIVITIES WITH A BUDGET CALENDAR

A budget calendar is prepared to permit participation in the actual preparation of the budget by as many school employees as possible, yet recognizing the absolute need for organization, an orderly process, and the importance of one individual accepting responsibility for the total process.

While the beginning of the actual budget process may vary from school district to district, it is generally agreed that the final approval date by the board of education coincides with the end of the current school term and immediately prior to the date established by state law for submission of the budget to the state department of education (often June 30). A sample calendar is displayed in Figure 3.4 with accompanying activities.

	1992–93	1993–94			1994–95			1995–96		
Revenue	Estimated	Total	Increase	Percent	Total	Increase	Percent	Total	Increase	Percent
Subsidy	5,122,667	512,267	0	0	5,225,120	102, 453	2.0	5,381,874	156,754	3.0
Real estate	8,343,122	867,854	333,732	4.0	10,375,122	1,698,268	19.6	11,821,498	1,446,375	13.9
Wage tax	1,438,141	1,481,285	43,141	3.0	1,555,349	74,064	5.0	1,633,117	77,767	5.0
Transfer	243,018	243,018	0	0	253,018	10,000	4.1	268,018	15,000	5.9
Interest	330,200	345,200	15,000	4.5	360,200	15,000	4.3	375,200	15,000	4.2
Total	18,269,611	18,773,186	303,380	1.3	20,789,138	2,015,952	10.7	22,620,848	1,831,709	8.8
Expenditures										
Salary	9,815,313	10,674,153	858,840	8.7	11,560,108	885,955	8.3	12,253,714	693,606	6.0
Benefits	2,582,862	2,711,235	128,373	5.0	2,947,827	236,593	8.7	3,136,951	189,123	6.4
Debt serv.	974,032	960,763	(13,269)	−1.4	967,588	6,825	.7	962,235	(5,353)	−.6
Computers	130,000	150,000	20,000	15.4	150,000	0	0	180,000	30,000	20.0
LAMP	352,500	444,970	92,470	26.2	3,333,840	(111,130)	−25.0	265,533	(68,307)	−20.5
Other	4,679,093	4,824,145	145,052	3.1	5,022,900	198,755	4.1	5,274,045	251,145	5.0
Total	18,533,800	19,765,256	1,231,466	6.6	20,982,263	1,216,997	6.2	22,072,477	1,090,215	5.2
Unfunded balance		992,080			193,125			(548,370)		
Net mill value 147666		153,573			159,716			166,104		
Mills required		6.46			1.21			−3.30		
Total millage 56.5		65.0			66.21			65.91		

Figure 3.3 Three-year budget projection.

	1997–98
October 16	Curriculum meeting to address budget procedures.
October 21	Budget request forms disseminated to building administrators, support staff supervisors, curriculum coordinators, and central office administration. (Directions for computer accessing will be included.)
October 24 (Act 80 dismissal)	Department/grade-level chairs share budget information with staff.
November 27	Letter of intent sent to professional staff by building principal (return by Monday, December 2)
December 2	Principals submit to superintendent enrollment forecast by individual building.
December 11	Review of elementary and middle school staffing additions and reductions.
December 12	Projection of facility needs is due.
December 13	Business manager projects to superintendent revenue side of budget.
January 3	Grade-level and department chairpeople submit prioritized budget requests to building principals.
January 13	Principals and directors submit prioritized budget request forms to business office.
January 27	Superintendent, business manager, and director of
February 3	instruction meet with supervisors and principals to review budget requests.
February 10	Principals review revised budgets with curriculum
February 14	coordinators.
February 24	Review of staffing at all levels.
February 26	Principals meet with superintendent and business manager to review adjusted budget requests.
March 3 March 10	Superintendent and business manager place budget into format for presentation.
March 10	Board of education projects salary percentages for classified, teaching, and administrative staffs.
March 10	Board of education finance committee reviews revenues for budget.
April 3	Board of education reviews initial budget in budget conference session.
April 28	Board of education's second budget review.
May 19	Tentative approval of budget by board of education.
June 23	Final approval of budget by board of education.

Figure 3.4 Sample calendar.

REVENUE PLANNING

As stated earlier in this book, it is important that as budgeters are developing their educational and expenditure plans they also develop a revenue plan. Essentially, this means predicting how much revenue can be expected from federal, state, and local sources. Usually this activity determines any increase to be sought in local revenue if the prediction for total revenue does not fund the proposed budget. See Budget Example, pp. 95, 97–99, 105–106.

FEDERAL REVENUES

Of late, federal revenue has been easy to predict, as it is specific to programs and is usually allocated on specific bases such as need or expenditure in areas of federal concern, for example, nutrition or reading. Recently, total revenue from federal sources has been stable and also quite low, usually below 3% of a district's total revenue, with less than 1% not uncommon.

STATE REVENUES

Revenue from state sources is another story altogether. It is apt to vary widely from state to state and district to district, is based on a variety of methods even within a state, is more difficult to predict than federal revenue, and is often a substantial percentage of a district's budget, in some cases over 80%.

Districts should as accurately as possible develop their own methods of determining their state revenue as part of the budget development process. This often causes central office administrators, particularly superintendents and business officials, to establish networks for gathering information about what is happening in the state capital.

Predicting State Revenue as an Art Form

In states where local school districts rely on the state legislature passing its budget as a determiner of a major source of the district's revenue, predicting when the legislature will act is almost as much of a problem as guessing what the state will dole out. As districts must have their budgets in place by a particular date, it becomes interesting, at the very least, estimating revenue from state sources. Developing your district budget is not unlike shooting at a moving target from a hammock! Some administrators and board members have contacts in the state legislature who can be counted upon to accurately assess the direction the legislature will ultimately take and, more specifically, what that direction means for their district.

If you don't have good contacts at the seat of state government (often an anatomically accurate metaphor), or your elected representative is the junior member or a member of the minority party, or is not interested in public education, or for any other reason doesn't know what is going on, you would be wise to cultivate relationships with your peers who have an almost artistic ability to know what the folks in Capital City might do. Every area of the country has its board members, superintendents, or business managers who can make a call and determine an accurate prediction of what form the legislature's generosity will take. District budget makers should be able to reach out and touch these artists.

Associates in your networking, particularly elected representatives or bureaucrats, should be contacted on other subjects and at other times, not just about state subsidies at budget time. As many writers on the subject of communicating with elected officials will tell you, it is important to keep in touch with these people. Call them to express thanks for their help or to support, not just to oppose, proposed legislation. Help them in data gathering for their projects. The latter is also a service you should provide educators in other districts.

Your system for planning revenue from the state should include several alternative scenarios, given the normal course of events when dealing with the state: mainly unpredictability and inadequacy of money. You should develop courses of action against the twin possibilities that (1) the state will provide you less money than you need and (2) you will be informed of this after you have adopted your budget.

LOCAL REVENUES

One major factor in estimating local revenue is the historical record of collection for each local tax in the school district. The district's business office should maintain annual records of dollars raised per unit of tax and the percentage of taxes collected each month. The latter is of value in managing cash flow, predicting revenue for budgeting purposes, and predicting interest income. When local revenue is being estimated, budget makers should know, for example, the amount a mill of property tax can be expected to bring in on average. The budget developers then can predict how that historical number can be expected to rise or fall due to current economics. Factors such as housing starts, business and industry climate, unemployment rate, age of the work force, as well as the tax rate help in gaging each tax will bring to *the district budget* revenues in any given year.

It is helpful for board members and others using the budget to know what kind of information went into building that budget. Consequently, prose or tables in the budget showing what economic factors were used and how they were weighted, as well as tax collection rates and dollars received/unit of each tax, should be part of the budget document, not just part of the process.

The individuality of revenue problems from district to district places great emphasis on the need for local planning. The resulting plans have to include contingencies against the possibility that, for whatever the reasons, a forecast turns out to be less than accurate. Although, perhaps not as mercurial as the stock market, local economic conditions can change quickly, and their effects, even when conditions do not change, are not always accurately predictable.

ROAD MAP OF PRIORITIES

The annual budget, which is in essence the operating plan for a single year, functions as a road map for all district activities and programs. As such, it is a statement of what the organization values and, thus, its priorities (see Budget Example).

The budgeting process must be an ongoing and organized program. While state statutes set forth various requirements and district boards of education may select specific dates for activities, budgeting is a year-round project. The major summary activities in the budget process are by nature analytical and preparatory and are usually completed by the administrative staff regardless of the degree of decentralization. This work may not have specific time lines in that it is compiled on a continuous basis.

Boards of education want to know when the administration will present summaries of budgetary requests, when board committees can begin to review requests, when the tentative budget will be presented to the board, when the public has the opportunity to review the budget, and the time line for the board to have final discussion and adopt the budget (see Figure 3.5). Boards are normally not interested in the details of budget preparation, unless they are in the habit of micro-managing.

WHOSE RESPONSIBILITY?

As the reader can discern from the budget calendar, the activities to be completed include all levels of staff but are directly related to the responsibilities of the district administrative staff. Board members must be able to question the effects and impacts of recommendations. In addition they have to know the

Board Meeting Dates	Budget Function Dimensions to Be Reviewed
February 6, 1999	3000 Operation of non-instructional services 4000 Facilities acquisition, construction, and improvement services 5000 Other financing uses Available revenue information
March 16, 1999	1000 Instruction Available revenue information
April 20, 1999	2000 Support services Available revenue information
May 4, 1999	Expenditure update, revenue, tentative adoption
June 15, 1999	Adoption (proposed)

Executive sessions of the board will be scheduled for discussion of confidential matters such as personnel.

Figure 3.5 Public development schedule for the 1998–99 budget.

priorities of the district through strategic plans, vision statements, etc. and must receive valid information. The school board member, particularly one who is not a professional educator or financier, must rely on the district administration to direct the activities and provide control over the resources.

It is the responsibility of the board, however, to (1) ask for recommendations in areas where they lack expertise, (2) pose questions to gain an understanding of concepts and details, (3) compare budgets from previous years with the one under discussion, and (4) insist that the budget reflects the short- and long-term goals and priorities of the district.

The superintendent, usually as a commissioned officer of the state, provides leadership and direction to the budgetary process. It is his/her responsibility to assist the board in its efforts to be responsive to the local community's needs and to provide an effective financial plan. Whether a program is instructional or non-instructional, the superintendent assists the board in evaluating its importance to the education of children (see Figure 3.6).

Note in the partial example shown in Figure 3.6 that the superintendent is not mentioned because in this hypothetical case he or she provides leadership, including oversight, for the entire budget-making process.

The business manager is the source of factual data, which should be timely and accurate for budget preparation. This individual must possess the ability to communicate the bottom lines to the superintendent and board and must be able to work closely with the superintendent in any planning process.

There is a "horror story" still circulating among school administrators who enjoy dazzling each other with tales of prowess and bad luck (never stupidity or good luck) of the superintendent who, through an oversight

(1997–98 Budget).

Budgetary area	Responsible staff member
Instructional supplies	Principals
. . .	. . .
Library books	Library/media chairperson
. . .	. . .
Musical instruments	Music chairperson
. . .	. . .
Salaries	Business manager
. . .	. . .
Textbooks	Department chairpersons Elementary principals
Transportation	Director of transportation

Figure 3.6 Sample budget responsibility chart.

in the responsibility area, left out an entire section of the budget when it was presented to the board for adoption. The section was administrative salaries and, according to legend, the board was reluctant to help the superintendent out of his mire but, rather, told him to find the money elsewhere in the existing budget proposal or not pay administrators that year.

This story has doubtless been embellished over the years, and its ending has since been lost. It is, however, a scary warning to budgetary leaders: make certain every area of the budget has someone responsible for shepherding it through the development process.

BOARD HOLDS FINAL RESPONSIBILITY

While the answer to the question of who makes the final decision regarding programs and activities to be included in a budget is apparent, in that the board of education is the authority in any school organization, the discussion and dynamics that occur in any entity are frequently site specific and thus vary both in degree and intensity.

Currently, many school districts are using some form of decentralized budgeting or site-based procedures while others remain highly centralized in their approach to the actual building of the annual budget (see Budget Example). The authors have used and espouse an eclectic approach from a variety of viewpoints: that is, promote participation wherever possible and appropriate, use zero-base concepts where they are practical, etc.

1997–98

Math
Home Economics
Pupil Services

1998–99

Social Studies
Music
Special Education

1999–2000

Library/Media
Foreign Language

2000–2001

Science
Power Technology
Health/Physical Education

2002–2003

Language Arts
Business
Art

Figure 3.7 Proposed curriculum cycle.

CURRICULUM RENEWAL CYCLES

While, as indicated above, it is frequently a "spitting into the wind" process when attempting to provide the board of education and the community with a long-range budget plan, the utilization of a 5-year cycle in organizing curriculum revision is critical and most helpful.

With a curriculum renewal plan, those individuals building budgets attempt to level the financial demands for curriculum renewal from year to year. Figure 3.7 demonstrates how all instructional disciplines are reviewed and brought current through the scheduling of a 5-year cycling plan.

It must be noted that the teaching staff is most enthusiastic about the curriculum cycling, as they recognize that all instructional disciplines "have their turn" to revise curriculum, purchase resources such as textbooks, software, etc. and thus renew the instructional process.

MERIT PROPOSALS

The use of the merit proposal concept also deserves attention in the overall budget process. With this procedure a fixed amount of money can be placed into the budget annually to fund program areas that are recognized and agreed upon to be of high priority.

Currently, the area of technology, that is, purchasing of hardware and software, lends itself well to this concept. Using the form in Figure 3.8, teachers submit to the district's director of technology (through the building principals) projects to be evaluated and rated or prioritized.

Those projects or activities receiving the highest rating points or priority are funded until the stipulated sum of money is depleted. In this way, meritorious projects can be realized and those staff who address district priorities and goals are rewarded and supported.

A DOCUMENT TO ATTAIN VISIONS

With the concept of strategic planning or long-range planning, a well-conceived educational program and the means for implementing the educational activities becomes more easily attainable. The budget document, then, is merely a plan, a statement of programs and services—with prices attached—to achieve the visions and goals of the educational organization.

VISION: A technology program infused successfully into the instructional, administrative, and community educational programs to provide knowledge and skills necessary for success both today and in the future.

The purpose of the "Technology by Proposal" process is to continue to express and expand upon our district's technology vision. Through the use of staff-designed proposals, technology will continue to be infused into instruction and further implement the reforms education is realizing as we move forward into the twenty-first century.

The evaluative criteria used in proposal selection consists of the following: numbers of students affected by the proposal, curriculum impact of the proposal, and clarity and completeness of the description for implementation. The reviewing committee will make every effort to evenly fund proposals throughout the district.

Completing the Proposal

1. Indicate the building being represented in the proposal.
2. Name every staff member involved in designing and implementing the proposal. One or more staff members may present a single proposal. If more space is needed for additional staff, please attach a separate sheet to complete the list.
3. Name the place(s) where the proposed technology will be based.
4. List every item needed to complete the proposal. Indicate how many of each item are being requested. Include hardware, software, peripherals, and support or incidental items (carts, power strips, etc.)
5. In the narrative, use a clear and concise style to describe infusion of the technology into the curriculum. Add information pertaining to the student population destined to benefit from the proposal. Include the outcomes expected to be realized by the use of the technology in the curriculum.
6. Complete the remaining pages accurately and neatly.
7. Turn the completed forms in to your building principal no later than Wednesday, January 17, 1996.

Figure 3.8 1996–97 technology merit proposal guidelines.

Building	Fort Zeller	Myerstown	Middle School
	Schaefferstown	Jackson	High School

Submitted by:

Teacher _____________ Grade _____ Department ____________

Teacher _____________ Grade _____ Department ____________

Teacher _____________ Grade _____ Department ____________

Teacher _____________ Grade _____ Department ____________

Teacher _____________ Grade _____ Department ____________

Planned location of the technology: ______________________________

List the specific items you are requesting:

Quantity	Name/Description
____________	________________________________
____________	________________________________
____________	________________________________
____________	________________________________
____________	________________________________
____________	________________________________
____________	________________________________

Clearly describe how the requested items will be used in the curriculum. Please list the expected outcomes.

____

____

____

____

____

____

____

When completed, submit the form to your building principal.

__________________________ ______________

Principal's signature Date

Figure 3.8 (continued) 1996–97 technology merit proposal guidelines.

While we have addressed somewhat the significance of the budget process being a participatory one, the school community must realize that decisions are never made in isolation or by one individual. The mission of the district as well as its visions are foremost, and support of the board and the various staffs of the district for programs for achieving the visions is vital to the overall success of the plan.

PRIORITIZING OF REQUESTS

While the budget becomes a monetary statement of district priorities and policies, the board and the administration team must balance competing demands to produce a document that formally addresses the instructional needs of the community's children.

It is most helpful to structure the budget process through the use of standard forms, organization, and a system of prioritizing budgetary requests. However, these should be standardized within a district; they may be individualized for each district to achieve "what works for us."

Indeed, the form depicted in Figure 3.9 illustrates a request format that can be used by teaching staff and that includes prioritizing by the teacher, the department or grade-level chair, and the building principal. It must also be noted that informal as well as formal discussion among staff are part of the prioritizing that is so critical to the decision- making process.

LEVELS OF PRIORITY

The prioritizing activity cannot be overemphasized when evaluating budgetary requests. Frequently the prioritization is completed by using a three-level system such as indicated below:

(1) Priority #1: The funding of this request is mandatory, as the equipment, supply, etc. is essential to attaining a district vision or goal. Priority #1 also includes requests critical to health, welfare, and safety of staff and students.
(2) Priority #2: The funding of this request should be realized, as the equipment, supply, etc. addresses a clearly understood need.
(3) Priority #3: The funding of this request is not required but is desirable, as the equipment, supply, etc. enhances the total program.

What may occur in the use of this zero-based system is that staff will declare that all requests are of priority #1 when completing the budgetary request form. What a blow to the system! The only "correction factor" available is for supervisors and principals to then complete their prioritizing through questioning of

TOTAL COST PLUS SHIPPING $51.28

			Priority
BUDGET CATEGORY	610 SUPPLIES		Teacher 1
QUANTITY · 10	DESCRIPTION Pencils Item #183902	VENDOR & ADDRESS Office Supplier 100 Main Street Any town, USA	Curriculum Coordinator Principal
UNIT PRICE #3.95			COST $ 39.50

CATEGORY SUBTOTAL (Cost Plus Shipping) $45.42

			Priority
BUDGET CATEGORY	610 SUPPLIES		Teacher 2
QUANTITY 1	DESCRIPTION Scissors Item #38290409	VENDOR & ADDRESS School Supplies, Inc. 200 First Street Your City, USA	Curriculum Coordinator Principal
UNIT PRICE $5.09			COST $ 5.09

CATEGORY SUBTOTAL (Cost Plus Shipping) $5.85

Figure 3.9 Proposed budgetary requests (1997–98).

staff who submitted the original request and by relying on their own knowledge of the importance of the request to the overall educational program.

Superintendents, principals, business managers, boards, and community taxpayers realize that resources are not unlimited. Although faculty realize this too, they sometimes forget that it also applies to them. (You can easily discern that your authors are or were superintendents of schools.) The challenge in budgeting remains, therefore, to provide quality programs with limited resources!

LETTER OF INTENT

In that personnel and their accompanying benefits comprise approximately 70% of a school district's budget, it is wise to survey staff early in the school term (perhaps November) with a Letter of Intent (see Figure 3.10). In this manner financial savings can be anticipated through attrition, leaves of absences, etc.

To: Professional Staff

From: Superintendent of Schools

Re: Professional Intent for 1997–98

Date: November 14, 1996

In planning the budgeting/staffing needs for the 1997–98 school term, we need an indication of your plans with respect to your position in the school district for the upcoming year. **Please return this form to your building principal by Thursday, November 28, 1996. (Note: This does not commit you to your response but is merely used for our tentative planning.)**

Thank you.

______ I plan to return for 1997–98.

______ I would like to discuss reassignment for 1997–98.

______ I will be retiring.

______ I will be requesting a sabbatical leave. (All sabbatical leave requests must be submitted to the Board of Education by February of the year prior to the leave.)

______ Other (Please specify) ______________________________

____

____

____________________ ____________________

SIGNATURE OF EMPLOYEE BUILDING

Figure 3.10 Letter of intent.

CONTINUOUS DEVELOPMENT

The annual budget development stems from the concept of continuous budget development; that is, immediately upon adoption of a budget, work begins on the formulation of next year's fiscal plan.

Strengths and weaknesses in the operation of the current budget are evaluated, and educational plans are conceived on a multi-year or long-range basis. With this continuous development or year-round principle put into practice, the educational staff as well as the board of education are given adequate time to consider an addition or deletion on the basis of educational merit and cost.

To implement this concept, discussions must be scheduled throughout the year by administration, by teaching staffs, and by the board of education. Tickler files which prod individuals to reflect, think about, and make suggestions concerning the budget are also valuable. Establishing a calendar of activities and events that occur over a twelve-month period is most critical, as is the mandating of reports to spur study of items that should be considered in the budget.

GENERAL ACTIVITIES

This year-round concept can best be illustrated with the following budget time lines:

- planning—July through December
- preparation—January through March
- deliberation—April through June
- adoption—June
- execution—July through June
- evaluation—July through December

THE BUDGET DOCUMENT

The budget development process will result in a large document that will be used throughout the year by many people. Budgets are no longer merely a few pages of numbers used by almost no one once they are adopted. Rather, they tend to be multiple-page, public-planning documents utilized often by educational and business administrators, board members, teacher leaders, the media, community leaders, and many other planners.

The budget can and should be used in staffing, purchasing, scheduling, accounting, controlling, staff development, organizing, and general planning as well as general administration. School districts, through organizations for school business affairs, now compete for recognition of their budgets as to completeness, usefulness, and communication (see parts of a 265-page sample budget in the Budget Example).

Because budgeting is planning, and the budget is a planning document, budgets now include information helpful in understanding how the district is projecting and financing the expected results. The typical presentation of fiscal information now is communicated in multiple ways to assist the reader in understanding and using the information (see Figure 3.11).

SUMMARY

The budget process can be viewed as an equilateral triangle with the educational plan as its base (see Figure 3.12). If any one of the three sides is altered, the other two must also be changed. Only when the three sides meet does a budget document emerge.

Current, historical, and predicted revenue and expenditure figures
Description of the district
Mission statement
Goals
Staffing plans
Facility plans
Maintenance schedules
Strategic plans
The budget process
Curriculum cycles
Enrollment history and projections
Records of student performance
Organization charts
Directory of board and school personnel
Glossary

Figure 3.11 Subjects typically included in the annual budget.

This concept of budget development, then, assumes and requires that formulating the educational mission, visions, and goals of a school system is the first step in the process. From the visions and goals an educational plan results that is translated into a fiscal plan for presentation to the board of education and the community for reaction and possible adoption. With the discussions that develop, compromise results from what the community will support and what the school staff perceives as necessary for the children.

A functional budget does, of necessity, consider the educational plan prior to its consideration of the fiscal resources. By its very nature, it translates the quantitative and qualitative features of the instructional program into program expenditures and endeavors to demonstrate the needs so that the public will provide the required fiscal resources through taxes.

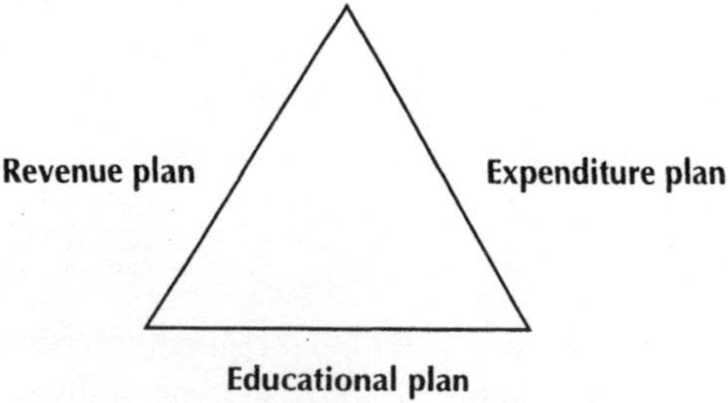

Figure 3.12

CHAPTER 4

Budget Approval and Adoption

THE process of approving the district's annual budget is especially critical and is frequently political. It requires patience, organization, prioritization, and a keen sense of timing on the part of the teaching staff, the administrative staff, and the board of education.

While politics plays an enormous role in the passage of the school budget, the overall goal of the process is to produce a financial plan that provides a quality education for children through utilizing limited financial resources.

The "war stories" that have evolved regarding budget feuds between the superintendent and the board of education are, for the most part, real. The reader only needs to review the declining average tenure of the superintendents across our country to realize that personality, budget fights, and politics are all interrelated and can cause the superintendent's flight or resignation.

Recently two board members in a highly affluent, suburban school district in Pennsylvania approached the superintendent and told him they would vote for his budget if he changed various programs contained in the budget. The response of the superintendent was that the budget was not for sale, nor was he, nor was the quality of education for the children of the district. The result was "loggerheads," anger, frustration, and probably a conflict that will never be resolved!

Nevertheless, the budget adoption process goes on and takes different roads in different school districts.

PLANNING FOR SUCCESS

As discussed in the previous chapter, prior planning of the educational program is paramount to successful budget adoption. The overall commitment to the instructional program through the formulation of written mission, vision, and goal statements makes the adoption process more tolerant, simplified, and perhaps even less political.

While there will always be an abundance of needs and more requests than resources, the prioritizing of the budget requests on the basis of the strategic or long-range plan and ultimately bringing the educational plan to fruition must be the rationale used in all budgetary discussions.

MODELS TO CONSIDER

The concept of the administration-dominated budget is waning. Furthermore, this centralized budget—wherein all schools within a system are treated as if they were only one—while it is a very efficient procedure in developing a budget, it permits little consideration for differing needs among the children served. In addition, the practice of allocating resources on a per pupil basis often gives no consideration to existing resources and fails to recognize the heterogeneous nature of diverse individuals.

Thus, the authors fully support a participatory method that rests on two principles: (1) schools that are tax supported must consult citizens in the budget process if they expect continuing support and (2) individuals involved in the daily operation of the schools, namely teachers, supervisors, etc., should be given the opportunity to request those resources and procedures that will enable them to perform their duties more effectively and efficiently. The approval process, thus, of necessity involves the entire school community.

Not all board members are a model of enlightenment. Rather, it is not unusual for administrators or other board members to find it necessary to ask questions or make statements in budget deliberations that point out that the budget is for the educational betterment of the students, all of the students. If one or two board members become political, parochial, or otherwise unstatesmanlike, a fellow board member can often provide a proper focus by asking, "How does that advance our program?" or "How will that benefit our students?" The superintendent or another administrator, by pointing out as subtly as possible how little the children benefit from the questionable behavior of adults, is often enough to get the majority of board members back on track. Unfortunately, it is often necessary for boards, with some pushing by the superintendent, to police unboardmanlike behavior.

A BOARD RESPONSIBILITY

Adopting the school district budget is one of the most salient responsibilities of the board of education. The fiscal plan, moreover, is a delicate balance of priorities, choices, and policies. The actual passage of the budget by the school board should signal the best possible educational program for the children of the school district and the best possible use of the available resources. Normally the administrative team and the board members have a comprehensive view of the variables affecting the budget and its adoption. However, the budget passage process should not take on a political or special-interest flavor. The approved fiscal plan must serve the needs and interests of all, not the chosen few.

While the superintendent of schools will usually occupy the pivotal role in the approval of the budget, all who have a part in its development assume roles in its passage, either negative or positive. If the budget formulation process is a democratic or participatory one and if communications throughout its development have been effective, the resulting document is never a surprise to the school community.

WHAT INCREASE WILL PASS?

A rule of thumb for the overall increase projected from budget to budget, barring significant annual changes in student enrollment, is the average rate of inflation for the year or the increase in the consumer price index. If the district has been planning effectively in a long-range mode, there is little rationale for a sharp jump in the bottom line of the budget.

Assuredly, student enrollment projections, planning for facility construction and renovation, and cycling the curriculum renewal process all contribute in a positive manner to the "leveling" of required budget revenues.

PRIORITIZING FOR APPROVAL

Teachers and other staff members participate in the budget formulation by submitting individual requests for supplies and equipment; thus, they have a vital stake in the adoption of the budget.

As these individual requests are prioritized (see Levels of Priority in Chapter 3) by the staff member and submitted to department chairs, grade-level chairs, or program supervisors for further prioritizing, those expenditures that address building and district goals receive approval for further consideration in the budget process. After the building principal has prioritized the requests and meets with the central staff to give further support where needed, the district staff presents to the appropriate board committees new or significant programs and expenditures for approval.

ADVISORY GROUPS

At times citizens may be involved as members of advisory committees or study groups. Attempts to involve teachers, other staff, and citizens can fail because of inadequate planning and a lack of role definition (decision making, commenting, etc.) for those participating. All who take part in the budget process must be made aware of the disposition of their proposals and, thus, the results of their efforts. In this way participation and feedback or communication give a better understanding of the district's mission, vision, and goals.

USE OF COMPARISONS

As the budget winds its way toward approval by the board of education, a helpful tool that often brings expenditures as well as total revenues into focus is the comparative data provided by state departments of education or regional educational agencies known as intermediate units, BOCES, and intermediate school districts (see Figure 4.1).

The total spectrum of the budget—for example, local, state, and federal resources; percentage of debt service in relation to the bottom line of the budget; dollars expended for pupil transportation, etc.—should always be examined thoroughly. Using the state averages or the intermediate unit average figures when examining broad categories of revenues and/or expenditures can often give the Board and community information that supports the budget plan or information that explains why the request for expenditures may appear unfounded (see Figure 4.2).

	District		State	
Highlights	Per Pupil Expenditures	Percent of Current Expenditures	Per Pupil Expenditures	Percent of Current Expenditures
Expenditures for current operations	$5,605	100.00	$6,068	100.00
Expenditure for total instructional services	4,088	72.80	4,266	70.31
Expenditure for total student services	450	8.01	539	8.95
Maintenance and operations	372	6.62	461	7.53
Environmental conditioning	192	3.41	146	2.36
Total staff compensation	4,339	77.28	4,640	76.18
Total revenue	6,453	100.00	6,442	100.00
Budget Profile—Detailed Information				
Total revenue	6,453	100.00	6,442	100.00
Local revenue	4,065	62.99	3,975	61.70
State revenue	2,216	34.34	2,379	36.93
Federal revenue	172	2.67	88	1.37

Figure 4.1 Budget comparisons (1993–94): district to state averages.

	District						
	A	B	C	D	E	F	G
Instruction (per pupil)	$3,536	$3,567	$3,693	$3,668	$3,367	$3,513	$3,542
Administration (per pupil)	$419	$469	$405	$374	$385	$350	$364
Special programs (per pupil)	$388	$323	$450	$381	$376	$325	$377
Operation/ maintenance (per pupil)	$486	$569	$505	$587	$408	$471	$558
Debt service (per pupil)	$62	$6	$541	$566	$463	$666	$194
Transportation (per pupil)	$200	$279	$286	$311	$201	$212	$57

Figure 4.2 Financial comparison study.

When examining the area of student activities, for example, it may be wise to compare your district's expenditure per pupil with that of your region and state. The same may hold true for the category of pupil transportation or guidance services.

PRESENTATION OF THE TENTATIVE BUDGET

When initially presenting the working budget to the total board of education in April, a useful technique is to begin with a visual presentation of total revenues projected, total expenditures, the tax increase proposal, and then various sets of comparative and absolute data, including but not limited to the following (see Figures 4.3, 4.4, 4.5 and Budget Example, pp. 83–87, 95–97, 105–118, 123–132.):

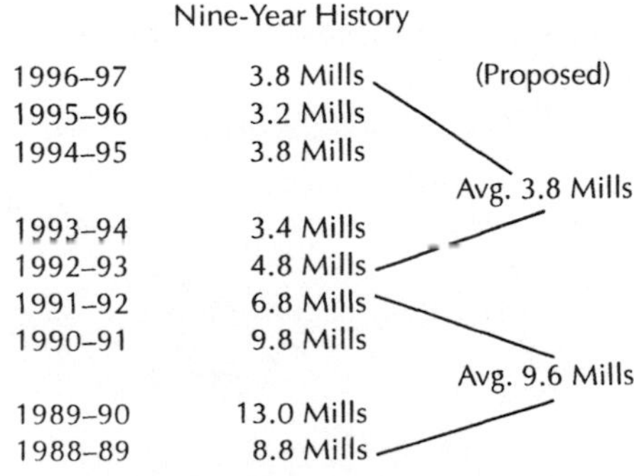

Nine-Year History
1996–97 3.8 Mills
1995–96 3.2 Mills
1994–95 3.8 Mills
(Proposed)
Avg. 3.8 Mills
1993–94 3.4 Mills
1992–93 4.8 Mills
1991–92 6.8 Mills
1990–91 9.8 Mills
Avg. 9.6 Mills
1989–90 13.0 Mills
1988–89 8.8 Mills

Figure 4.3 District millage increases.

Grade	Range	Average	Total
K	16–22	20	162
1	18–22	20	159
2	18–24	21	190
3	18–25	24	190
4	21–25	24	167
5	17–23	20	190
	Total		1058

Figure 4.4 Class sizes—student enrollments in elementary schools.

- average class sizes—by building, grade and/or department
- anticipated tax increases of districts in the region
- total current tax millage of districts in the region
- significant new programs included in the budget and their cost
- significant deletions in the budget and their overall effect on the millage required
- salient new expenditures such as the cost of the negotiated teachers' contract
- personnel changes
- revenue categories—local, state, federal
- divisions of expenditures—maintenance, instruction, etc.

At this presentation, it is most useful for the superintendent to have available for the board handouts that document various programs, full copies of the budget document, and, of course, administrative and supervisory personnel who can address specific questions. Accuracy is crucial to any successful development and presentation, and accountability for inclusion of applicable functions, programs, etc. is also very important.

IMPORTANCE OF BUDGET DEVELOPMENT

If the budget development process is completed effectively, the major questions to be answered will be few, and the most significant issue will be whether

Budget Year	Value of One Mill
1996–97	$68,500
1995–96	$66,500
1994–95	$64,900
1993–94	$63,041
1992–93	$61,500

Figure 4.5 Five-year millage history.

or not the community accepts the proposed increase as one that is fair and provides a sound educational program for its children.

TRUST AND CONFIDENCE

This "feeling" of the budget being fair and within the limits of the community is a matter of public trust and confidence among board members, the administrative and teaching staffs, and the public. For board members the "how to" of budgeting is not the critical issue in the adoption process. They do need to know, however, the district priorities and be knowledgeable as to the impact of recommendations. Confidence in the administration team goes a long way in the board being able to recommend the working budget for tentative approval.

AN INVISIBLE CEILING

It must be noted that the success or failure of the adoption process is frequently tied to the "invisible ceiling," which the board or community has established as the potential tax increase. We all have witnessed the turmoil that results and its shattering effect upon the entire school district when the proposed millage increase is out-of-line with neighboring school districts or with the zeitgeist of the community.

The repair of the school organization's credibility takes years and can often cause flight of staff and community alike from the district. The district that is adamant in its unwillingness to fund the educational program through a tax increase is perceived by parents and those outside the system as an ineffective school system. The district that does not plan properly to increase taxes by small increments or, conversely, that has "peaks and valleys" in its millage pattern is in store for a "rocky ride."

Administrators and board members who have "been around awhile" all know of districts that have little or no standing in educational circles. Unrest is common. Fiscal conservatives in the community are not alone in thinking education there is too expensive. Progressives don't think their children are getting the best education possible. These districts' reputations are such that better educators are reluctant to apply for their vacancies.

Rarely is the cause for this low esteem unknown. Often it seems to result, either directly or indirectly, from large, inconsistent fluctuations in taxes—often times no tax increase for 5 or 10 years, followed by several large increases. During the latter the conservatives scream, while the progressives are apt to scream during the former as well as the latter. After one or two of these cycles, no one respects these schools, and a general undercurrent of disharmony and dissatisfaction persists.

THE LOCAL BURDEN

Nationwide, public schools have witnessed the diminishing role of the federal government in the revenue arena. Even more devastating, however, has been the abdication by most state governments in assuming their share of responsibility for the funding of education. Thus, the brunt of the revenue production has fallen to the local taxpayer through the regressive property or real estate tax.

A SUICIDAL PLAN

This trend of decreasing federal and state funding makes budget adoption even more difficult in the suicidal tax-increase arena. Nevertheless, the one recommendation that your authors would give to you is, "*Do Not* under any circumstances give back or cut the local tax rate." The saga of local districts that have returned 1 or 2 mills in a year only to raise taxes 7–10 mills in the following year is legendary! The uproar and resulting resignation of the superintendent or board members is needlessly caused by this thoughtless action: the old adage of "what have you done for me lately?"

The mill or two returned is never, never remembered in the year of tax escalation. A much more prudent action would be to "bank" the 1 or 2 mills in a capital reserve account so that additional millage would not be required down the road for building repair or even construction. Even though this is the more sensible approach, some board members will view it as taking taxpayers money before it is needed.

A RECURRING PROCESS

Certainly the adoption of the budget signals that the process is complete. Nevertheless, with tentative approval the document must usually stand for 30 days for public review before final passage can be granted. With the final passage, the implementation of the new budget year begins.

FUND BALANCES

Two issues that have not been discussed yet deserve consideration at this point. The concept of fund balance—its use and its amount—often is debated publicly and becomes a major stumbling block to the budget approval process.

The term *fund balance* is used to describe the difference between assets and liabilities. When assets are greater than liabilities, the resulting balance is a positive one. The actual fund balance can include such items as money due but not received, for example, delayed federal payments.

WHY HAVE A FUND BALANCE?

School districts must retain monies in reserve to pay for emergency repairs or unexpected interruption in revenue sources, just as an individual or family establishes a savings account for unforeseen expenses. In addition to generating fiscal interest income, a fund balance is advantageous to a school district when a bond issue is required. The credit rating of a school district is usually affected directly by the level of the fund balance—those with little or no money in reserve are considered higher risks and their costs of borrowing or ratings are therefore higher.

During the budgeting process, a school district projects the unreserved fund balance for the next year. The purpose of the fund balance is to provide monies for the expenditures that have not been anticipated in the budget or be a cushion for anticipated revenues not received. The public position taken by critics is that school organizations have been "squirreling away" large sums of money in their fund balance and that these amounts have been growing; thus, additional tax increases and state aid cannot be justified.

The questions then arise as to how large should a fund balance be and for what purposes should it exist.

The balance sheet portion of the financial document shows that assets equal liabilities plus fund equity. The computation for fund equity is–in actuality–assets minus liabilities equals fund equity or fund balance. The fund balance, therefore, represents the difference between the fund's total assets and total liabilities.

The size of the fund balance changes during a fiscal period because of activities in primarily the revenue and expenditure categories: revenues increase the fund balance while expenditures decrease it.

Why do districts need a fund balance? The major reasons are (a) lack of or uncertainty in state funding, or its delay, (b) unforeseen emergencies, such as snow removal or boiler replacement, and (c) periodic large expenditures financed through a fund balance that has been accumulated for several years for this specific purpose. It must be noted that sufficient levels of unreserved fund balance contribute significantly to the stability of property tax revenues and the orderly operation of the educational organization.

FINANCIAL STABILITY

To ensure that a school district is financially stable, annual revenues should equal or exceed annual expenditures. For the short term, the fund balance, if at an excessive level, can be used as revenue, which will have the effect of increasing available monies and thereby reducing local taxes required to balance the budget.

If the district, however, uses the fund balance for recurring expenditures such as teacher salaries or utility expenditures, or if the district continues to use the fund balance annually to support current expenditures (and lower tax rates), the fund balance will diminish and require large tax rate increases. Additional taxes will also be needed to rebuild the fund balance to a previous level.

Once again the singular purpose of the fund balance is to provide monies for unanticipated expenditures or to provide for revenues anticipated but not received. After the school year has begun and taxes have been levied, the school organization does not have the opportunity to raise revenues for additional, unavoidable expenditures or for revenue shortfalls.

To establish a definitive formula or model addressing the appropriate level for a district's fund balance requires that the particular uses for the funds be analyzed. Most districts abide by two guidelines: the minimum amount to hold in fund balance is 3% of the total budget while the maximum should not exceed 10%. The other guideline is that the final balance should absolutely never be used for recurring expenditures such as personnel but can be used for one-time expenditures such as boiler repair or equipment purchase.

BUDGET COMPROMISE

From time to time a stalemate may develop in the adoption process, and a budget compromise may be necessary. In this case our experience clearly demonstrates that the relationship of the program and its expenditures to the visions and goals of the district should be the deciding rationale, if the total budget increase is within the confidence of the board–administrative team. In many of these instances it is wise for the superintendent to remember that there are some principles that cannot be compromised, the major one being, "We must do what is best for the children."

Compromise, although usually lauded, is not always in the best interest of education, and sometimes it is just plain wrong. Certainly board members in their political arena should be capable of compromise, and administrators are hardly in positions to be obstinate. Budgeters should not compromise ethics nor should they often give in to arrangements that cost more money in the long run. Priorities and plans may have to be adjusted to get a budget approved, but school leaders have to remember why they were selected for their positions.

SUMMARY

Adoption of the annual district budget is the final step in the democratic, participatory development process. The formal adoption is normally a two-step process, taking place within a 30-day period usually in May and June. Much of the success lies in the degree of credibility and confidence that the administrative team has been able to develop with the board of education and the community.

With the decrease in both the state and federal share of monies to public education and the resultant increase in the share that the local community must shoulder, the adoption process has entered a highly volatile arena. The reader only needs to follow the current problems in Ohio or New Jersey, with their reliance on property or real estate taxes for major revenues, to gain a perspective of the problems lying ahead for school budget passage, in particular, and public schools, boards of education, and superintendents, in general.

CHAPTER 5

Administration of the Budget

BUDGET ADMINISTRATION AND MANAGEMENT PROCESS

BUDGET administration and management is the process of regulating expenditures during the fiscal year to ensure that they do not exceed authorized amounts and that they are used for intended proper and legal purposes. The management of the budget is accomplished in a variety of ways: monitoring program implementation, controlling expenditures, tracking revenue receipts with effective and efficient purchasing procedures, making corrections in expenditure allocations to reflect changes in costs, service levels, or plans, and reporting to the board and public on fiscal operations.

The budget has been approved, and it is time to begin using the monetary resources that have been provided. Funds have been allocated to the departments in accordance with the plan. The superintendent will want to know if the district is financially healthy. Because a budget is a careful estimate of expenditures, it is wise to remember that no plan is going to be implemented without changes due to unforeseen conditions. You will want to be able to make adjustments in the budget as needed. During the preparation of the budget the document itself serves as the vehicle for planning and resource allocation decisions in the district. Now that the budget has been adopted it becomes the major fiscal management tool for administering and controlling expenditures. There are, however, other budget administration and management issues important to the budget process that are discussed below.

ORGANIZATION FOR BUDGET MANAGEMENT

The decision-making philosophy and organizational structure of the district for budgeting not only affect the planning and developmental phases of the budget, but they also affect the way in which it is administered and controlled.

Those districts in which the board and administration believe in a highly centralized budgeting method, having all important decisions made in the central office, will very likely administer and control a budget in the same manner. Many school districts today believe that decisions are best made at the lowest possible level in the organization. This has led to budget preparation and implementation becoming more decentralized and site based.

Commonly, the decision-making philosophy and organizational structure of the district combine elements of the management team and school-site management concepts. It is an approach between centralization and decentralization in philosophy and structure. Many of the decisions in the district are formulated by management teams with the responsibility for budget control at the building or department level (such as transportation or pupil services).

For example, the administrative cabinet, which is comprised of central office administrators, reviews and approves curriculum recommendations of the principals prior to presentation to the board for final consideration. Teams of administrators at the central office and teachers at the building level are thus an important part of the decision-making process for educational programs and curriculum in the district. Funds to support curriculum revisions are then monitored and controlled by appropriate cost-center managers.

The overall spending and revenue plans are coordinated by the central office to keep the districts total expenditures within available revenues. District-level coordination is also exercised in such areas as personnel policies, which are established and monitored centrally to maintain general uniformity and compliance with negotiated collective bargaining agreements and with state and federal statutes. However, budgetary allocations to responsibility cost centers, particularly the building budget appropriations, are provided in an unrestricted lump sum amount. Decisions on how to allocate these monies are made at the site or department level. For example, principals who have responsibility for cost centers provide participation for the professional staff in the decision-making process on the use of building resources. See Figure 5.1 for an expenditure requisition process.

- Department head/supervisor receives request for material, personnel, or service.
- Expenditure justified and budgetary constraints reviewed.
- Requisition approved by central office administration.
- Requisition sent to purchasing department for processing; purchase order created and mailed for materials or services.
- Material, service, etc., received by requesting department.
- Approved invoices sent to the business office for payment.

Figure 5.1 Expenditure requisition process.

EXPENDITURE CONTROL AND APPROVALS

For management control purposes and in order to execute the budget plan effectively, the operating budget (general fund) of the district is usually assigned to a number of responsibility cost centers. A budget manager (an administrator or coordinator such as a building principal or maintenance director) is accountable for the management of the financial resources approved by the board for each of these responsibility cost centers. These cost center managers should receive printouts of the budget allocations for which they are accountable as soon as the budget is officially approved. The printouts usually display the program name, classification of expenditure (salary, benefits, materials, contracts, equipment), budget allocation, amount expended, amount encumbered, and the unobligated balance. It is important in the budget control process that managers be responsible for their assigned budgets by operating within their limits and seeking approval for changes or additions before expenditures are incurred.

Effective budget control requires that the superintendent or other administrator vest budget authority in these cost center managers, hold them accountable for the funds allocated for them, and provide a framework for adjusting the budget when needed (see Budget Example, pp. 101–104, 116–117, 128–129). Most budgets have some margin built into them so that when a necessary unallocated expense does present itself, it can be absorbed. In a business that should be encouraging the innovative and constructive ideas of its employees, it doesn't make much sense to tell your staff they can only pursue ideas that were fully developed before the middle of the budget year. Solutions to problems should not be rejected because they were reached at the wrong time on the budget calendar and, therefore, do not have official funding.

TRANSFERS BETWEEN BUDGET ACCOUNTS

The budget is a spending plan based on a series of assumptions and estimates. Rarely, if ever, will all of the actual expenditures be equal to the detailed budget estimates. As actual expenditures are incurred, adjustments are required in the budget between accounts to cover higher than expected costs or to provide for an unanticipated expense. However, district controls on the transfer of funds ensure that expenditures do not exceed available financial resources. Usually the business manager or director of the budget office has the primary responsibility for monitoring and adjusting the financial plan during the fiscal year, subject to board approval.

Board members are usually much more supportive of administrative fiscally related recommendations if they understand the budget and know its status and

TO: Business Office

FROM: ________________

SUBJECT: Request transfer of funds in the amount of:

$----,----,---.--between the following two budget accounts:

From		To
-	Year	-
---	Fund	---
-------	Function	-------
-----	Object	-----
-	Level	-
---	Location	---
-------	Program	-------

Reason for transfer

Description (Use ONLY if a new accounts is to be established)

Principal or Director Date

Approved Date

Completed Date

Figure 5.2 Transfers between budget accounts.

relative evaluations such as where its accounts are compared to last year at this time why a transfer is needed now from account B to account A (see Figure 5.2).

ENCUMBRANCE CONTROL

Another important component in the district's financial control and reporting system is the encumbrance of funds. Encumbrances are obligations in the form of purchase orders, contracts, or salary commitments chargeable to an appropriation (for which part of the appropriation is reserved). The purpose for the encumbrance of funds is to ensure that obligations are recognized as soon as financial commitments are made. Otherwise, the accounting system would only record actual amounts entered into the expenditure accounts, not those that are planned or anticipated. In short, the encumbrance of funds is an important control measure to prevent the inadvertent overexpenditure of budget appropriations due to the lack of information about future commitments. For budgetary purposes, appropriations lapse at fiscal year end, and outstanding encumbrances usually must be paid within 90 days.

ONGOING EVALUATION OF THE BUDGET

The chief financial officer of the district is the main source of overall district financial information. This individual is charged with monitoring the overall financial health of the district and knows the "big picture." Expenditure and revenue patterns should be continuously examined, looking for trends, deviations from expected rates and costs, changes in levels of participation in programs, unbudgeted spending, and any other factors that have a bearing on obtaining and spending funds.

A wide assortment of data should be examined to probe the efficiency of the district's expenditures. Actual spending should be monitored against the budget and compared to prior years. Financial information, coupled with salary data from the personnel files, should be used to project salaries very accurately. Pupil population data and personnel counts from a position control system can give information on class loads that can be assessed against planning objectives.

By organizing and summarizing the systems information, the financial officer is in a position to provide accurate operational status reports on a regular basis. Periodically, this information should be assembled and published for a financial review. This review, in addition to providing timely information needed to keep the district on target with its operating plan, also is useful in keeping elected officials and the public aware of potential problems. Regular financial reviews show that you are planning and managing, not just reacting to events.

REPORTING ON FINANCIAL ACTIVITIES

A monthly financial report should be presented to the board of school directors for their approval and to the public for their information. Among the items to be included should be the following:

(1) All bank account balances and activity
(2) All investment activity
(3) All general fund, capital reserve fund, and escrow fund activity

(4) Line-item budget report summary
(5) End-of-month bills list and check register for previous month
(6) Regular bills list for current month
(7) Capital reserve fund financial report
(8) Dental clinic fund financial report
(9) Student activity fund financial report
(10) Food service department financial report

In addition to a monthly report, an annual financial report is usually required by the state department of education. In many cases and annual CPA audit is also required by the school code which includes federal programs. A state audit, usually conducted by the auditor general's office, may include a financial audit and program/school code compliance audit. This is normally done covering a two-year period, after which an audit conference is held with the board of school directors and superintendent.

USING AUDITS EFFECTIVELY

An audit is an important aid to good management and should help to instill public confidence in your administration. Audits will typically disclose any ineffective practices that may exist. Speedy actions should be taken to ensure that audit findings are appropriately addressed. Internal financial audits are an important way of ensuring that the appropriate records are being maintained and that an established procedure is being followed. They should be an ongoing process. The knowledge gained should be widely shared among district staff who have financial responsibilities to help improve their overall performance.

Audits performed by the district's CPA firm often include valuable advice in the management letter. Although these recommendations are just that and not mandates, they are frequently very helpful in the management of the district's financial operation and usually have budgetary impact. Consequently, the board should be informed of the status of all such recommendations, particularly those that the administration does not believe the advice can or should be taken.

INVESTMENT PROCEDURES AND CASH MANAGEMENT

The variable timing of receipts and disbursements can cause cash balances to accrue. This routine occurrence can be predicted with considerable accuracy, thus enabling you to take advantage of these opportunities to invest the funds (Figure 5.3). The district may want expert help in developing a policy for governing their investments because of the large amounts of money involved. The

Daily Investing of All Funds

Certificates of deposit
Bank money market accounts
Bank savings accounts
School district liquid asset fund
Local government investment
Trust fund

Daily Cash Management

Cash flow projections
Tax receipts monitoring
Subsidies administration
Cash needs

Payroll Procedures

Separate checking and savings accounts
Funded as needed

Figure 5.3

investment policy should include a careful screening of investment institutions such as banks and brokers. It should specify the minimum qualifications needed to do business with the district and the terms under which investments are made including the handling of collateral. The best policy will include bidding investments. Bidding investments are not required, but the policy should include a request for a proposal process. Bidding will help avoid making investments with low yields and also serve to blunt political maneuvering to favor one institution over others. Preservation of capital over return on investment should be stressed.

PURCHASING PROCEDURES

Good purchasing procedures can save the district many dollars. The procedure should include the following:

(1) A purchasing department that seeks to match the goods and services needed with reputable vendors who deal in the same goods or services and can provide the necessary services and warranties after the sale. Qualified bidders must be capable of acquiring a performance bond, making their facilities available for inspection, and delivering goods as promised on a consistent basis.
(2) A vendor bid list maintained for each category of goods and services
(3) Specifications for goods and services
(4) Utilization of state and local governments and agencies
(5) Cooperative purchasing with other governments and agencies
(6) Reviews of inventory to reduce or eliminate stock infrequently used
(7) Auctions to dispose of surplus equipment or materials

If expenditure will be more than $10,000:

(1) Request board permission to bid
(2) Prepare specifications and bid package
(3) Advertise and solicit bids
(4) Public bid opening and tabulation of bids
(5) Award recommendation to board and obtain board approval
(6) Prepare purchase order

If expenditure will be less than $10,000 but more than $4,000:

(1) Prepare specifications and quotation form
(2) Solicit at least three price quotations
(3) Review and tabulate quotes
(4) Prepare purchase order

Items exempt from bid requirements:

Service contracts, Professional services, Maps, Music, Globes, Charts, Films, Tapes, Discs, Textbooks, Games, Toys, Kits, Models, Demonstration devices, and Perishable items, Including food and beverage

Figure 5.4 Bidding process.

Purchasing is a specialized function that requires good business sense, honesty, and a knowledge of contracts (also see Figure 5.4).

School district purchasing is another one of those aspects of school business that is often different from the non-school world. Because schools should and do rely, where possible, on the advice of their professionals for budgeting and purchasing goods and services, there is often a conflict between the recommendation of employees and budgeting and purchasing (particularly bidding) procedures. Administrators should learn to walk the thin line between the views of quality expressed by a faculty or staff and the law or procedures to be followed in bidding and purchasing. It may not be possible or sensible to reject the low bid for blue paint because it is not "blue enough" for the art faculty while it may be possible and most sensible to reject the low bid for wax because your maintenance people can show it contains too much water to really be the least expensive.

YEAR-END EXPENDITURES

Large spending in the last quarter of the financial year is often perceived as indefensible and irresponsible by board members and the public. Sometimes managers purposely try to conserve funds throughout the year anticipating emergencies or changes in plans that superintendents and boards frequently impose during the year. From the cost center managers point of view, this is a survival technique that is not entirely without merit, given their experiences. It would be wiser to set up a central contingency fund early in the year and use it for emergencies and changes in the spending plan. The funds could be temporarily deployed from accounts that usually yield surpluses due to economic or consumption factors that the district has anticipated in a conservative manner. Tell managers that they are to proceed with spending as budgeted, but that it is to be weighted toward the early part of the year when most expenditures occur. Not all of the non-wage expenditures can follow this plan, but partial adherence can result in reduced last-minute spending.

Cost center managers are also concerned that unexpended funds will result in reduced future allocations. If budgets are padded, certainly reductions are in order. However, if a surplus occurs as the result of unforeseen conditions, such action is not necessary. Unforeseen circumstances during the financial year may cause large sums of money to accumulate. This should not be viewed as negative, although the reasons for this happening should be determined and preventive actions taken in future budgets. A plan should be prepared for the use of the surplus, and because it is not a recurring source of funds, one-time purchases such as equipment or maintenance projects should be considered for funding. It is also possible to increase the appropriated fund balance to support next year's budget.

PLANNING FUND BALANCES

The general expectation on the part of the public and sometimes the board members is that most things are predictable with a high accuracy a year in advance, and, therefore, no surplus should be available. Veteran administrators are aware that no budget plan will be spent exactly as forecast. A carefully prepared budget surplus is the natural result of a rational spending plan as allocations place a top limit on spending.

It is important to anticipate a fund balance and take action to include it as a source of funds in future budgets. The Pennsylvania School Boards' Association advocates a fund balance of 5–6%. Wise use of it should be made recognizing its variable nature.

SUMMARY

Budget approval is only the first step in ensuring that the school district is able to implement a quality educational program for students. It is wise to recognize that the budget document is not a static, unchanging reflection of school district needs and priorities. It is one that changes and requires supervision, projecting, analysis and evaluation, the movement of funds between accounts, and auditing at the end of the fiscal year.

As the budget year proceeds, it is the responsibility of the financial officer to keep the cost center managers apprised of the status of funds remaining, trends developing, or available alternatives and options. It is not the responsibility of the financial officer to substitute his or her judgment in managing the educational process but to maintain their office in a service role.

Successful administration of the school budget is one of the high-priority duties of the administration. It is a cooperative process requiring a constant flow of information throughout the organization. With appropriate budget preparation and budget administration tasks defined and implemented, the staff will have insured for the students of the school district their educational program.

CHAPTER 6

Budget Example

THIS section is drawn with permission from a recent budget of the Council Rock School District, an 11,000+ student, K–12 district in suburban Philadelphia.

This is not the complete budget but, rather, sample pages and sections included as examples. Ellipses (. . .) indicate one or more of the following pages have been purposely omitted.

Council Rock's budget is relatively program oriented. Because it relates to programs and is a document that is used throughout the year, much of the information included is to provide residents and educators of the district with information that is helpful in understanding how the budgetary process works in Council Rock and how the district is planning for the future.

ENROLLMENT PLANNING

Pages 119–122 give some indication of budgetary procedures that deal with enrollment change and projection.

HUMAN RESOURCE AND FACILITIES PLANNING

This is a growing district that clearly recognizes its need for planning, particularly in the areas of human resources, facilities, and programs. Space does not permit the inclusion of budget pages showing the planning process for human resources and facility planning. Suffice it to say pages omitted show planning for these two areas similar to that shown for enrollment. Pages 115–118, 122, 123, 133, however do show some information used in or resulting from facilities planning.

STRATEGIC PLANNING

The Commonwealth of Pennsylvania mandates strategic planning for all of its 500 school districts. Strategic planning results lead to changes in expenditures and, consequently, should be part of a program budget. Pages 89 and 133–134 document the role of strategic planning in this budget.

STUDENT ACHIEVEMENT

Modern budget documents should show student progress. Page 82 and addresses this topic.

BUDGET DEVELOPMENT PROCESS

The process of building the budget in Council Rock is described on pages 95–97.

REVENUE AND EXPENDITURE

Typical revenue and expenditure pages from the budget are shown on pages 97–132, and a commentary on measuring available revenues and expenditures is on page 95.

DISTRICT STRUCTURE

A description of the district's history and composition appears on pages 92–94.

BUDGET EXAMPLE

The actual sample budget follows.

July 31, 1996

Dear Board Members,

The budget (and subsequent expenditures) of a school district is the financial expression of the school board and the administrative staff's educational priorities and policies. One of the objectives of regulatory reporting and financial accounting in a school system is to provide clear and concise financial reports to the public as a basis of judging past, present, and future priorities and policies.

Existing state and agency forms and regulations dictate the appearance of a school district budget. These established formats result in financial presentations that are in compliance with state and local statutory and regulatory mandates but frequently are not in a form that provides a basis for judging past, present, and future priorities and policies by the public. The public generally views the school system in a very practical and uncomplicated manner. They simply want to know the answers to a few basic questions such as:

1. How well are our students achieving?
2. Where does the money come from that we use to run our school district?
3. How much money will we spend to run our school district?

A basic premise of this summary is to report 100 percent of the costs of running the Council Rock School District. Therefore, the data contained in this summary is based upon all funds that are used by the District to finance the expenditures during the budget year. It may also serve as an ongoing management reporting format and communication tool for the parents, educators, businesses and taxpayers involved with the teaching and learning of the children of the Council Rock School District.

Another basic premise is that our students are indeed learning and achieving very well as confirmed by data presented in this summary.

Sincerely,

Charles A. Scott

Dr. Charles A. Scott
Acting Superintendent

(1) How well are our students achieving?

- 33 Council Rock High students are nominated to participate in the 1997 National Merit Scholarship Program.
- 12 Council Rock High students are 1996 National Merit Finalists.
- Newtown Junior High student is selected as one of the top 150 high school math students in the country on the American Invitational Math Exam.
- Council Rock Mathletes team won Annual High School Mathematics Contest at Millersville University.
- Rolling Hills Elementary student, one of 68 nationally, achieved a perfect score in the Wordmaster Challenge (Gold Division), a national language arts competition.
- Hillcrest Elementary student, one of 171 students nationally, received a perfect score in the Blue Division of the Wordmaster Challenge.
- Newtown Junior High student is a finalist for the USA National Computer Programming Team.
- Standardized battery testing scores for the district at the elementary level received an average national percentile score of 89 for 94–95 year, which falls in the "well above average" classification.
- Council Rock High students were winners in seven of the nine categories of the Bucks County Foreign Language Oral Proficiency Contest.
- 71 seventh grade students from all three junior high qualified for a "Certificate of Excellence" for their performance on the Scholastic Aptitude Test.
- Holland Junior High seventh grade won second place in PA Mathematics League Competition.
- 170 students district wide participated in the Bucks County Reading Olympics.

(2) Where does the money come from that we need to run our district?

1996–97 District-Wide Revenues
Council Rock School District

	Total Dollars	Percent of Total
Total funds	$105,582,008	100.0%
Total projected enrollment—11,910		
Local sources—real estate taxes	64,158,736	60.8
—Earned income Taxes	6,450,000	6.1
—Other taxes	9,234,757	8.7
—Other sources	2,444,448	2.3
—Total	82,287,941	77.9
State source	23,126,097	21.9
Federal sources	116,920	0.1
Other sources	51,050	0.0

(3) How much money will we need to run our school district next year?

1996–97 District-Wide Expenditures by Fund
Council Rock School District

	Total Dollars	Total per Student
General fund	$107,515,517	$9,027
Athletic fund	463,267	39
Capital reserve fund	3,301,657	277
Total	$111,280,441	$9,343
Total projected enrollment—11,910		

(4) How much money will we spend on each major function next year?

1996–97 District-Wide Expenditures by Function
Council Rock School District

	Total Dollars	Percent of Total	Total per Student
Instructional purposes	$68,849,175	61.9	$5,781
Instructional support	9,635,341	8.7	$809
Operations	15,126,847	13.6	1,270
Administration	5,589,730	5.0	469
Other commitments	12,079,348	10.9	1,014
Total	$111,280,441	100.0%	$9,343

(5) What proportion of funds will we expend at the school and district levels?

1996–97 District-Wide Expenditures
Council Rock School District

	Total	Schools	District and Non-Allocated
Instructional purposes	61.9%	57.4%	4.5%
Instructional support	8.7	4.6	4.1
Operations	13.6	4.9	8.7
Administration	5.0	3.7	1.4
Other commitments	10.9	0.0	10.9
Total	100.0%	70.5%	29.5%

(6) How much money will we allocate district-wide to specific personnel and supply needs?

1996–97 District-Wide Expenditures
Council Rock School District

	Total Dollars	Percent of Total	Total per Pupil
Instructional purposes			
Personnel and benefits	$66,780,234	60.0%	$5,607
Supplies and equipment	2,068,941	1.9	174
Total	68,849,175	61.9	5,781
Instructional support			
Pupil support	4,212,023	3.8	354
Teacher support	2,863,302	2.6	240
Program support	2,560,016	2.3	215
Total	9,635,341	8.7	809
Operations			
Non-instructional student services	5,338,513	4.8	448
School facilities	8,405,534	7.6	706
Central support services	1,382,800	1.2	116
Total	15,126,847	13.6	1,270
Administration			
Principal services	4,040,514	3.6	339
Superintendent services	1,045,662	0.9	88
Board services	503,554	0.5	42
Program management			
Total	5,589,730	5.0	469
Other commitments			
Capital expenditures	1,943,984	1.7	163
Debt service	6,061,608	5.4	509
Non-public transportation	2,698,256	2.4	227
Community services	25,500	0.0	2
Budgetary reserves	1,350,000	1.2	113
Total	12,079,348	10.9	1,014
Total	$111,280,441	100.0%	$9,343

(7) How much money will we allocate between school sites and central offices by major function?

1996–97 District-Wide Expenditures by Function and Location
Council Rock School District

	Schools	Central Offices	Non-Allocated	Total
Instruction				
Total dollars	$63,844,412	$1,316,394	$3,688,369	$68,849,175
Per pupil dollars	5,361	111	310	5,781
Instructional support				
Total dollars	5,075,272	1,126,759	3,433,310	9,635,341
Per pupil dollars	426	95	288	809
Operations				
Total dollars	5,492,343	5,713,701	3,920,803	15,126,847
Per pupil dollars	461	480	329	1,270
Administration				
Total dollars	4,086,085	1,503,645	0	5,589,730
Per pupil dollars	343	126		469
Other commitments				
Total dollars	0	0	12,079,348	12,079,348
Per pupil dollars			1,014	1,014
Total dollars	$78,498,112	$9,660,499	$23,121,830	$111,280,441
Total per pupil dollars	$6,591	$811	$1,941	$9,343

(8) How will we distribute this money among school levels by function?

1996–97 District-Wide Expenditures by Function and School Level
Council Rock School District

	Elementary	Junior High	High School	Out-of-District	Total
Instruction					
Total dollars	$33,227,665	$16,363,152	$13,658,594	$595,000	$63,844,412
Per pupil dollars	2,790	1,374	1,147	50	5,361
Instructional support					
Total dollars	2,077,529	1,685,705	1,312,039	0	5,075,272
Per pupil dollars	174	142	110		426
Operations					
Total dollars	1,624,201	1,201,835	2,666,307	0	5,492,343
Per pupil dollars	136	101	224		461
Administration					
Total dollars	1,891,340	974,017	1,220,728	0	4,086,085
Per Pupil dollars	159	82	102		343
Other commitments					
Total dollars	0	0	0	0	0
Per pupil dollars					
Total dollars	$38,820,736	$20,224,709	$18,857,668	$595,000	$78,498,112
Number of students	6,436	2,846	2,628		11,910
Total per student	$6,032	$7,106	$7,176		$6,591

Mission Statement
of the
Council Rock School District

AS A LEADER IN EDUCATIONAL EXCELLENCE,
IN PARTNERSHIP WITH THE COMMUNITY,
COUNCIL ROCK SCHOOL DISTRICT
IS COMMITTED TO CHILDREN
AND WILL EMPOWER THEM WITH SKILLS AND KNOWLEDGE
THROUGH COMPREHENSIVE, INNOVATIVE,
AND DIVERSE EDUCATIONAL EXPERIENCES, ENABLING THEM TO
ACHIEVE SELF-FULFILLMENT AND TO BECOME PRODUCTIVE,
RESPONSIBLE CITIZENS
WHO CONTRIBUTE TO THE WORLD COMMUNITY.

STRATEGIC PLAN

During the 1991–92 school year, the Council Rock School District reviewed the strategic planning process to assess the feasibility and value of the process in order to provide the impetus and framework for change and revitalization. Due to the increasing expectations of society that schools be responsible for many aspects of child nurturing, the school district realized that a comprehensive plan must be clearly identified fully meet the challenges of the future.

The primary concept states, "strategic planning is the means by which an organization constantly recreates itself to achieve common purpose." A basic premise of this definition asserts that change is not the result of accident or coincidence but occurs through careful planning and deliberation by a cross section of the organization who will benefit from the outcome. In fact, the strategic planner believes the future is presently "unmade" but will be made exactly as people make it. Strategic planning is a process designed to identify, with employee and community input, a district's mission and beliefs and then develop plans to work toward those beliefs through a focused planning process.

Implicit in this definition is the total commitment of all efforts, resources, activities, and energies toward a single goal. Dissension or priority differences by those who comprise the organization will result, at the least, in the wasteful use of resources, and, at most, will prevent the organization's ability to successfully achieve its goals. "Strategic planning in not political manipulation—not by the school board, not by the superintendent, not by the teacher union or any other special interest group within the school system or the community. Planning cannot be predicated on hidden scenarios and ulterior motives. It is not a time for competition. It is not an occasion for bargaining or power plays."

At the September 8, 1992 meeting of the Council Rock School Board, members of the board voted unanimous approval for our district to begin the strategic planning process. Working together, we envisioned a plan that would encompass all functions of the district and would allocate available resources toward the successful realization of the plan's goals. The 1994–2000 District Strategic Plan was approved at the November 19, 1993 meeting of the Board of School Directors for immediate implementation.

To successfully accomplish the plan's strategies, policies, and objectives, there must be a partnership between the school district and the community. Today, more than ever, it takes a "whole village" to educate a child. It is equally important to understand that learning is a lifelong process. The primary goal of the school system is to produce responsible citizens with the necessary skills to become capable, contributing members of a changing society.

Budgetary Implications

Annually, the district selects goals that are consistent with the strategic plan and the curriculum goals of The Pennsylvania Department of Education. The goals may be generally stated to maintain the quality of the educational program or specific action plan objectives as identified in the strategic plan. The action plan objectives and goals provide direction to the school district for the allocation of available resources.

After considerable review and evaluation of the goals and objectives by the district administration, the goals and objectives are formulated into a proposed budget document, which is proposed to the Board of School Directors for review and consideration. The budget is proposed at a public meeting in April and adopted in May. Opportunities are provided for community input and questions on the proposed budget.

ASSUMPTIONS, GOALS, AND OBJECTIVES

General

To maintain the mission of the district during 1996–97, the funding shall support expenditures with the following assumptions to meet long-term objectives and short-term goals against which to measure performance.

Assumptions

(1) Enrollment—The district foresees a three percent (3%) annual growth in enrollment, causing the number of children to reach 11,900 within the 1996–97 school year.

(2) Facilities—No new buildings will be occupied during the year. Several projects to repair or add to existing school buildings will be given urgent attention. Additional modulars will be installed to provide additional classroom space at three schools. Work will begin on the construction of a middle school and an elementary school. Office space requirements for the central administrative services will be evaluated and may lead to Board decisions and additional current expenditures. All expenditures for these actions will be accounted for in a Capital Reserve Fund and funded through long-term debt instruments.

(3) Mandates—No major changes in state mandates are expected during the school year.

(4) Staffing—The curriculum at all levels will be reviewed to ensure that children are provided with learning experiences essential to personal

development, responsible citizenship, and lifelong learning for the twenty-first century. Hiring policies and performance appraisals will emphasize demonstrated ability to facilitate a child's learning.

(5) Compensation—Permanent employee compensation will be according to agreements signed with CREA, CRESPA, and CRAA, which continue in force during the year.
(6) Organization—A Superintendent, plus additional administrative staff, will be recruited to provide improved efficiency in managing day-to-day operations.
(7) Revenues—State subsidies and reimbursements are forecast to continue to show a decline. Demand for local revenues has risen by more than seventy percent (70%) over the past 5 years.
(8) Transportation will show a decline in expenditure by utilizing the bus fleet more economically.
(9) No new curricular initiatives will be implemented if desired current educational programs are not funded.
(10) A modest number of action plans to continue the implementation of the strategic plan will be initiated.
(11) Expenditures in all line accounts will be reviewed to determine where needed economies can be made.
(12) A comprehensive program of educational and support services is required to maintain the standard of excellence established in the Council Rock School District.

Objectives

(1) Emphasize the agreed upon needs of children in all decision making.
(2) Maintain and improve community support for public schools.
(3) Require high expectations for quality performances and develop comprehensive assessment practices for all permanent employees.
(4) Recognize and reward job performance.
(5) Demonstrate fiscal responsibility by using public funds wisely.

Goals

(1) Appoint a superintendent with vision, experience, and integrity.
(2) Plan for the twenty-first century by considering the future needs in curriculum, technology, facilities and staffing.
(3) Assign permanent staff with an emphasis on classroom duties.

(4) Install and operate an integrated, single-entry, distributed computer-based, administrative record-keeping and reporting system.
(5) Prepare board policies and update administrative procedures that guide the more important activities.
(6) Improve communications with all parties in the district.
(7) Question how to maintain quality schooling at acceptable cost.
(8) Review all contracts and amend those not serving the district well.
(9) Review the strategic plan and report on progress to date.
(10) Adopt a long-range financial plan.

DISTRICT STRUCTURE

The Council Rock School District was formed by state law and began operation on July 1, 1969. Located in lower Bucks County, covering an area of 72 square miles, with a population of 60,000 (1990 census) living in the five municipalities of Newtown Borough, Newtown Township, Northampton, Upper Makefield, and Wrightstown, it provides public schooling for more than 11,000 children.

The district is a political subdivision of the Commonwealth created to assist in the administration of the General Assembly's duties under the Constitution of Pennsylvania to "provide for the maintenance and support of a thorough and efficient system of public education to serve the needs of the Commonwealth."

The district is governed by a board of school directors, one from each of nine regions elected to four-year terms on a staggered basis every two years. The Board decides issues by public vote and has the power and duty to establish, equip, furnish, maintain, and operate elementary, secondary, and other schools required to provide schooling for persons living in the District between the ages of six and twenty-one who may choose to attend.

In financial matters, the district is a legally autonomous and fiscally independent body. The laws of Pennsylvania give the district corporate powers that distinguish it to be legally separate from the Commonwealth of Pennsylvania and any of its political subdivisions (e.g., local municipalities, counties). The Board has the power to determine the district's budget; to modify that budget; to approve expenditures consistent with the budget; to set tax rates, levy taxes, and establish charges; and to obtain capital funds for the school construction via bonded debt. These powers may be exercised without the approval of any other government agency.

The Pennsylvania Department of Education provides a general oversight relevant to fiscal responsibility, which includes an approval process that is compliance oriented and is more ministerial than substantive in character.

The district has nine elementary schools (grades K–6), three junior high schools (grades 7–9), and one high school (grades 10–12). It also is one of four sending districts to a vocational–technical school for high school students. Elementary school attendance places emphasis on the neighborhood grouping of school population, though to obtain the best balance of classes per grade in each building, at times municipal lines have to be crossed.

The program of studies for the elementary grades is designed to emphasize teaching a child to read with understanding, to compute accurately, and to express ideas clearly. The District's goal is to attempt to fulfill each student's LEA; students are grouped heterogeneously for the regular education program.

The junior high school instructional program is designed to meet the needs, interests, and abilities of students during early adolescence. A variety of courses and activities are available for each individual student to provide those learning experiences required to bridge the continuum between the elementary and high school. Course offerings permit students to explore many general areas, rather than specialize in narrow fields of study, to provide a broad background, which should be helpful to the student in high school and later in life.

The high school offers a program of courses to represent a flexible and comprehensive curriculum that provides major programs of instruction for both college-preparatory and general-education students, Programs of studies are available through a variety of elective courses in art, business, home economics, health, industrial arts/technology, and music.

Secondary school students may choose to attend the Middle Bucks Vocational Technical School in either half-day or full-day programs of occupational education that can prepare them for higher education or immediate employment at the time of high school graduation.

The District provides special education programs for students with special mental or physical challenges that affect their ability to learn readily from the regular instructional programs. In addition, more than 2000 students with exceptional academic ability are provided more demanding instruction in a variety of classes at all levels above the second grade. On the secondary level, honors and advanced-placement classes are offered in English, science, social studies, and mathematics.

To develop special individual talents, interests, or growth through involvement in organized group activities, students are encouraged to benefit from the many school-sponsored activities outside the instructional programs. Competitive athletics, band and choral programs, as well as a variety of clubs and organizations are available in these extracurricular activities.

With the assistance of the Bucks County Intermediate Unit #22, the district provides staff development of many kinds aimed at personal development and an improvement in the quality of learning in the District made possible by the discussion of educational ideas.

Area residents and representatives are also involved in the district through the Partners in Education program. This program encourages and promotes an exchange of human resources between our schools and community. Those community-based activities include service organizations, parent forums, drug and alcohol awareness, and volunteer programs.

Fund Structure and Accounting

The accounting system of the school district is organized on the basis of funds. Each fund is considered a separate accounting entity, with a set of self-balancing accounts that comprise its assets, liabilities and fund balance/retained earnings, and revenues and expenditures/expenses. School district resources are allocated to and accounted for in individual funds based upon the purpose for which they are to be spent and the means by which spending activities are controlled. The fund classifications used by the school district have been defined by generally accepted accounting standards that include three broad categories: governmental, proprietary, and fiduciary.

Resources segregated into the Governmental Fund category are those used for the usual school services financed by local taxes, state subsidy, and federal aid. The district uses two types of Governmental Funds: a General Fund and Special Revenue Funds (the Capital Reserve Fund and the Athletic fund). The General Fund is the operating fund of the School District. Special Revenue Funds are maintained to account for the proceeds of specific revenue sources that are legally or administratively restricted to expenditures for specified purposes. The Capital Reserve Fund is restricted to expenditures for capital items and debt service. The Athletic Fund is restricted to expenditures for athletic activities.

Resources segregated into the Proprietary Fund category are those used to finance activities similar to those often found in the private sector. The activities are usually financed, at least partially, from a user charge. The district uses only one Proprietary Fund: an Enterprise Fund (the Food Service Fund). The Food Service Fund is used to account for all revenues, food purchases, costs, and expenses pertaining to food service operations, which are financed and operated in a manner similar to private business enterprises where the stated intent is that the cost, including depreciation and indirect costs, of providing goods or services to the students on a continuing basis are financed or recovered primarily through user charges.

Resources segregated into the Fiduciary Funds are those held by the school district as a trustee or agent for some other entity or group. The district uses two Fiduciary Fund types: Trust Funds and Agency Fund. Trust Funds are used to account for scholarship funds held by the district in a custodial capacity and include both expendable and nonexpendable trusts. The district accounts for the Education Foundation as both Nonexpendable and Expendable Trust

Funds. The Agency Fund is used to account for the receipts and disbursements of monies from student activity organizations. These organizations exist at the explicit approval of and are subject to revocation by the district's governing body. This accounting reflects the district's agency relationship with the student activity organizations.

The district is legally required to adopt budgets for the General Fund and all Special Revenue Funds. While not legally required, the district adopts a budget for the Enterprise (Food Service) Fund as a means to control expenses. The district is not required and does not adopt budgets for Fiduciary Funds. The General Fund budget, the Special Revenue (Capital Reserve and Athletic) Fund budgets and the Enterprise (Food Service) Fund budget are presented in this document.

Basis for Measuring Available Revenue and Expenditures

The modified accrual basis of accounting is used for the governmental fund types. Under this system, revenues are recognized when susceptible to accrual—both measurable and available. Available means collectible within the current period or soon enough thereafter to be used to pay liabilities of the current period. Expenditures are generally recognized when the related fund liability is incurred, except for principal and interest on general long-term debt, which is recognized when due.

Property taxes are recorded as assets when levied. Because the collection of those unpaid at the end of the fiscal year is not assured, they are recorded as deferred revenue rather than revenue. This deferred revenue becomes revenue in the fiscal year in which the taxes are collected. Property taxes collected within sixty (60) days subsequent to year end are susceptible to accrual under the modified accrual basis of accounting and are recognized as revenue in the current year.

The accrual basis of accounting is utilized by the Proprietary Fund. Under the accrual basis of accounting, revenues are recognized in the accounting period earned, and expenses are recognized in the period incurred.

. . .

BUDGET DEVELOPMENT PROCESS (1996 97 SCHOOL YEAR)

The budget process includes the following steps: planning, preparation, adoption, implementation, and evaluation. The process is driven by two objectives—to provide every child in the district with the best possible educational opportunities and to maximize the use of available resources. Within this framework, the board attempts to balance the educational needs of students and the resources available to the district from local, state, and federal sources. The product, the school district's budget that details the revenues and expenditures to support educational programs and services, is a delicate balance of policy choices.

Budget Planning

For the fiscal year that begins July 1, the planning process begins the prior September as enrollment, demographic, strategic plan, curricular, and revenue information are gathered. This information forms basic assumptions to be used by the Administration in developing basic budgetary guidelines. In addition, these assumptions form the basis for the Finance Committee's development of the Budget Calendar, including areas of inquiry and review, presentation, and justification.

Preparation of the Operating Budget

The preparation of the budget is the process of defining service levels such as the course offerings in the educational program; projecting student enrollment; developing staffing allocations; estimating expenditure needs to support programs and services; and projecting available revenues. The process begins when the Director of Elementary Education provides a forecast of elementary and secondary enrollments to the Finance Committee. The forecast of enrollments establishes an important assumption on which per pupil expenditure appropriations, instructional staffing allocations, and service levels such as the number of course sections and the number of transportation vehicles are based.

Central Office staff prepare pupil allocations for texts and supplies based on projected student enrollment. Meetings are then conducted with administrators and coordinators to review budget guidelines and formats. Building and coordinator budgets are due the first week of January.

The per pupil appropriations are established early in the budget cycle to permit staff involvement in the determination of resource allocations within the buildings.

This also permits the acquisition of supplies, materials, and equipment at the lowest price through the public bidding process and timely delivery of purchases prior to the opening of the school term. The budget process continues in accordance with the time line established by the Finance Committee. (Please reference the Budget Preparation Schedule.)

Since salaries and fringe benefits constitute approximately three-quarters of budget expenditures, the board gives careful consideration to staffing allocations for both instructional and non-instructional positions to provide for defined service levels.

The professional staffing needed to support the educational program is a function of the projected student enrollment, course offerings, and program needs. The staffing needs of the district are constructed on a zero-based approach at all levels. Proposed additions are carefully reviewed.

Preparation of the Capital Budget

The budget development process for the Special Revenue Funds, which include the Athletic Fund and the Capital Reserve Fund (the capital budget), proceeds concurrently with the foregoing process for the development of the operating budget.

The district is developing a Capital Reserve Fund Plan that provides for the maintenance of facilities. Projects are prioritized based on resolution of safety matters, compliance with state and federal statutes, maintenance of existing facilities, and improvements to buildings. In developing the plan, the board considers recommendations from the architectural consultants, insurance providers, the appropriate principal and director, (Maintenance, Business Affairs, Human Resources, Elementary Education, Secondary Education, or Special Services), and the Facilities Committee.

The critical elements in the development of the athletic budget are the estimation of program needs and gate receipts for ticketed events. The difference is the contribution required from the operating budget to support the extracurricular and athletic programs.

REVENUE CLASSIFICATION: *6000 LOCAL REVENUE SOURCES*

6111 Current Real Estate Tax

Real estate tax is the main source of revenue for funding the operation of the Council Rock School District. It is based on the assessed valuation as determined by the Bucks County Board of Assessment of all taxable property within the School District and is collected through a bank-operated lock box.

6112 Interim Real Estate Tax

Interim taxes are levied under Act 544 of 1952 (Section 677.1) on the increase in assessed valuations of local property as a result of construction or improvements to that property during the school year.

6113 Public Utility Realty Tax

Lands and structures owned by public utilities and used in providing their services are subject to state taxation under Act 66 of 1970. The state collects and then distributes a prescribed sum among local taxing authorities including school districts and that payment of state tax is in lieu of local taxes upon public utility realty.

6114 Payments in Lieu of Current Taxes—State/Local Reimbursement

Revenue received in lieu of taxes for property withdrawn from the tax rolls of the school district for public housing, forest lands, game lands, water conservation, or flood control. This revenue is classified as local although payments may be received from any one of several state agencies.

6120 Current Per Capita Taxes

Revenue received from per capita taxes levied under Section 679 of the Public School Code. A per capita tax is a flat rate tax levied upon each adult within the taxing district. The tax has no connection with employment, income, voting rights, or any other factor except residence within the district.

6141 Current Act 511 Per Capita Taxes

Revenue received under Act 511 for per capita taxes assessed. A per capita tax is a flat rate tax levied upon each adult within the taxing district. The tax has no connection with employment, income, voting rights, or any other factor except residence within the district.

6143 Current Act 511 Occupational Privilege Taxes

Revenue received under Act 511 for flat rate assessment of occupational privilege taxes. The occupational privilege tax is levied on resident and nonresident individuals employed within the taxing district for the privilege of engaging in an occupation.

6151 Earned Income

Earned income taxes are levied under Act 511 of 1965 (Local Tax Enabling Act) at the rate of one-half of one percent (.5%) of wages, salaries, commissions, net profits, or other compensation of those who earn income and reside within the school district.

. . .

EXPENDITURE CLASSIFICATION BY FUNCTION

The district uses four (4) major functional classifications to record and control financial transactions. However, expenditures are not charged directly to these major functional categories described below but to subaccounts or subfunctions that provide a more detailed classification of expenditures.

1000 Instruction

Activities dealing directly with the teaching of pupils or the interaction between teacher and pupils. Teaching may be provided for pupils in a school classroom, in another location, and in other learning situations. It may also be provided through some other approved medium. Included in this function are the salaries for teachers and assistants of any type that provide support for the instructional process. Also included in this function are equipment and supplies directly related to instruction and the instructional process.

2000 Support Services

Services that provide administrative, technical, personal, and logistical support to facilitate and enhance instruction. Support services exist to sustain and enhance instruction rather than as entities within themselves. They include such services as pupil personnel, guidance, psychology, library, health, attendance, business services, maintenance, and transportation.

3000 Operation of Non-instructional Services

Activities concerned with providing non-instructional services to students, staff, or the community. Expenditures accounted for in this function include student activities and community services.

5000 Debt Service and Other Financing Uses

Other financing uses represent the disbursement of governmental funds not classified in other functional areas that require budgetary and accounting control. These include debt service payments (principal and interest) and transfers of monies from one fund to another such as fund transfers to the Special Revenue Funds to support the Athletic Fund and the Capital Reserve Fund.

EXPENDITURE CLASSIFICATION BY OBJECT

The district uses nine (9) major object classifications to record and control financial transactions. However, expenditures are not charged directly to these major object categories described below but to subaccounts or subobjects that provide a more detailed classification of expenditures.

100 Personnel Services—Salaries

Gross salaries paid to employees of the district who are considered to be in positions of a permanent nature or hired temporarily, including personnel substituting for those in permanent positions.

200 Personnel Services—Benefits

Amounts paid on behalf of employees; these amounts are not included in gross salary, but are in addition to that amount. These fringe benefit payments, while not paid directly to employees, are part of the cost of personnel services.

300 Professional Services

Services that by their nature require persons or firms with specialized skills and knowledge. Included in this classification are fees paid to the Bucks County Intermediate Unit for special education services.

400 Purchased Property Services

Services required to operate, repair, and maintain property used by the district. Such costs include housekeeping, lawn care, maintenance, and snow removal.

500 Other Purchased Services

Amounts paid for services not provided by district personnel but rendered by organizations or personnel, other than Professional Services and Purchased Property Services. Such services include those for contractual agreements to transport students.

600 Supplies

Amounts paid for material items of an expendable nature that are consumed, worn out, or deteriorated in use. Such costs include textbooks, instructional supplies and materials, and energy costs for electricity and heating.

700 Equipment

Expenditure for the purchase of fixed assets. Such expenditures include initial equipment, additional equipment, and the replacement of equipment.

• • •

EXPENDITURE CLASSIFICATION BY COST CENTER

For management purposes for expenditures to meet the objective that they remain within approved annual budgets, the General Fund Budget is separated into Cost Center Budgets, each being the responsibility of a building principal, a central office Director or Coordinator, or the Superintendent. The responsibility cost center budget, especially the individual school budgets, may include several different functional areas. Although the annual expenditure for employees' salaries and benefits is found in the cost center budgets, responsibility for them is assigned to the Director of Human Resources.

Each of the thirteen (13) schools is a cost center with budgets assigned by object to determine the maximum annual expenditure that the principal can accumulate through contracted services, purchased supplies and materials, and employee expense reimbursement, etc. Budgets are assigned by function and object. The expenditures must stay within these individual levels.

COUNCIL ROCK COST CENTERS: *ELEMENTARY SCHOOLS*

Each elementary school is a cost center with the building principal being responsible for its budget. Funds are allocated for the following expenditures:

general instructional supplies and textbooks, audio-visual equipment, maintenance, library books, and for the supplies, postage, and other items required for school administration in the principal's office.

There are presently nine elementary school cost centers:

School	Principal	Projected Enrollment
Churchville	Mr. Michael Reid	852
Goodnoe/Chancellor St.	Mr. Harry Fritz	988
Hillcrest	Mr. Chris Cresswell	771
Holland	Mrs. Maryann Kline	663
Newtown	Mr. Mark Klein	754
Richboro	Mr. David Hunter	824
Rolling Hills	Mr. Tom Walsh	693
Sol Feinstone	Mr. Robert Winters	583
Wrightstown	Mrs. Fran Gelb	308

SECONDARY SCHOOLS

Each junior high school and high school is a cost center with the building principal being responsible for its budget. In addition to the principal, the junior high schools (grades 7–9) have an assistant principal, and the senior high school (grades 10–12) has five assistant principals. Funds are allocated to these four schools for the following expenditures: general and instructional supplies, textbooks, library books, new and replacement equipment, equipment maintenance, teacher conferences, field trips, and for the supplies, postage, and other items for school administration.

There are presently four secondary cost centers:

School	Principal	Projected Enrollment
Holland Junior	Mr. Mark Collins	986
Newtown Junior	Mr. Barry Desko	1,108
Richboro Junior	Dr. Joe Zaleski	752
Council Rock High School	Mr. David Yates	2,628

ADDITIONAL COST CENTERS

The following additional cost centers control expenditures within budgets for a variety of support functions.

District Services

The District Operations Budget provides funds for operating expenses of several district support offices. Among the budget items are district-wide health benefits, district library services, tuition to area vo-tech education, legal services, transportation, data processing, expenses of the board treasurer and board secretary, business office, human resources, and student activity accounts. Also included in this budget are tax collection services, debt service, property and liability insurance, fund transfers, and the budgetary reserve. The Director of Business Affairs is responsible for most portions of this cost center budget.

Special Services

The Special Services budget contains all accounts relating to student services provided apart from the regular education program. Special Education, Child Accounting, Instructional Support, Guidance Services, Free and Reduced Lunch Services, Psychological and Evaluation Services, Social Work Services, and School Nurse Services comprise this cost center. The Director of Special Services is responsible for all Special Services costs except for School Nurse Services, which is under the direction of the Director of Elementary Education.

District—Elementary

Almost all expenditures in this cost center pertain to salaries. Supplies, textbooks, homebound instruction, health services, and some superintendent costs are also listed here. The Director of Elementary Education is responsible for the cost center.

District—Secondary

In this cost center most expenditures pertain to salaries, as in the elementary cost center. Additional costs include career education, alternate instruction, textbooks, supplies, and superintendent costs. The Director of Secondary Education is responsible for the cost center.

District—Curriculum

Curriculum coordinator costs, temporary salaries (substitutes), technical services, travel, textbooks, dues and fees, the guidance department costs, some library services, and health services make up the expenditures in this cost center. The Director of Elementary Education is responsible for this cost center.

Staff Development

As students are encouraged to be lifelong learners, so then should all district employees be encouraged. Through staff development, positive changes will be evident in our schools and therefore reflected in our students. Staff development is a continuous process in which all Council Rock administrators, professional staff, and support staff gain and refine the skills and knowledge necessary to meet the ongoing needs of the profession and students. Staff development will assess and support the needs identified by the school district, the individual buildings, and the staff.

Participation in department approved in-service courses, curriculum development work, and professional conferences is encouraged and supported by the school district. Support is provided through the budgeting of funds and the granting of professional leave or release time for professional development above and beyond the school year. The school district recognizes in-service course work for salary purposes upon the issuance of a Masters' Equivalency Certificate. The budget for this cost center includes teacher salaries, general supplies, travel expanses, and registration fees. The Director of Elementary Education is responsible for this cost center.

Federal, State, and Local Grants

The federal, state, and local programs deal with exterior funding sources that support the spending in a variety of programs that include the Eisenhower Grant, Chapter II monies and carryover funds, Bucks County Drug and Alcohol Grants, Drug Free Schools, L.I.N.C.S. subsidies, and other extra grants. The drug and alcohol elements of these programs are the responsibility of the Director of Pupil Services. All other programs fall to the Director of Elementary Education's oversight and control.

District Maintenance

The cost center's funds include salaries, technical and professional services, snow removal, custodial services, some construction services, and supplies and equipment for the maintenance department, as well as utility costs such as disposal, extermination, and fuels expenditures. The Director of Maintenance is responsible for the cost center budget.

• • •

General Fund Revenue Budget

Function		1995–96 Budget	1996–97 Budget	Percent Increase
	Local Sources			
6111	Current R/E taxes	$62,375,650	$64,158,736	2.9
6112	Interim R/E taxes			
6113	Public utility realty tax	835,000	958,720	14.8
6114	Payments in lieu of taxes	300	400	33.3
6120	Current per capita taxes	184,175	196,991	7.0
6141	Pre capita taxes	184,175	196,991	7.0
6143	Occ. privilege taxes	100,000	120,000	20.0
6151	Earned income taxes	5,000,000	6,450,000	29.0
6152	Occ. taxes—millage	3,931,088	4,111,656	4.6
6153	R/E transfer taxes	1,600,000	1,600,000	
6400	Tax delinquencies	2,000,000	2,050,000	2.5
6510	Interest	1,817,403	2,242,458	23.4
6700	Student activities	23,000		−100.0
6910	Rentals	2,000	4,750	137.5
6930	Sales of equipment			
6940	Tuition from patrons	62,000	48,000	−22.6
6990	Misc. revenues	5,000	5,000	
Total Local Sources		**$78,119,791**	**$82,143,701**	**5.2%**
7000	**State Sources**			
7110	Basic instructional subsidy	10,475,680	10,471,263	−0.0
7160	Tuition (sec 1305 and 1306)	68,000	15,000	−77.9
7170	Instructional support teams	29,000		−100.0
7210	Homebound instruction	1,000	1,500	50.0
7220	Vocational education			
7271	Special education	3,341,007	3,515,537	5.2
7310	Transportation	1,950,000	2,144,555	10.0

(*continued*)

Function		1995–96 Budget	1996–97 Budget	Percent Increase
7320	Sinking fund payments	693,434	1,160,981	67.4
7330	Mental and dental services	22,000	15,467	−29.7
7340	Nurse services	202,000	215,259	6.6
7500	Extra state grants	7,500	15,000	100.0
7810	Social security revenues	2,075,000	2,133,459	2.8
7820	Retirement revenues	3, 393, 963	3, 438, 075	1.3
Total State Sources		**$22,258,584**	**$23,126,097**	**3.9%**
8000	**Federal Sources**			
8513	ECIA—Chapter 1	$198,425	0	−100.0
8560	Fed. block grants—Chapter 2	40,000	37,000	−7.5
8570	Eisenhower M&S subsidy		23,920	
8670	Drug free schools	57,000	56,000	−1.8
8690	Other restricted grants			
Total Federal Sources		**$295,425**	**$116,920**	**−60.4%**
9000	**Other Financing Sources**			
9330	Capital projects fund transfer			
9370	Trust and agency fund transfer		800	
9400	Sale/loss of fixed assets		250	
9500	Refund of prior years exp.		50,000	
9610	Receipt from other PA LEAs			
Total Other Financing Sources		**0**	**$51,050**	
Total Revenues		**$100,673,800**	**$105,437,768**	**4.7%**

General Fund Summary Expenditure Budget (by Function)

Function		1995–96 Budget	1996–97 Budget	Percent Increase
Revenue				
6000	Local sources	$78,119,791	$82,143,701	5.2
7000	State sources	22,258,584	23,126,097	3.9
8000	Federal sources	295,425	116,920	−60.4
9000	Other sources	0	51,050	
	Total Revenues	**$100,673,800**	**$105,437,768**	**4.7%**
Expenditure				
1100	Regular education	52,542,044	55,176,253	5.0
1200	Special education	13,192,669	14,995,301	13.7
1300	Vocational education	660,000	595,000	−9.8
1400	Other instructional	327,269	98,520	−69.9
	Instructional Programs	**$66,721,982**	**$70,865,075**	**6.2%**
2100	Pupil services	2,905,109	3,034,057	4.4
2200	Instr. staff services	2,591,054	2,454,700	−5.3
2300	Administration	5,281,517	5,589,730	5.8
2400	Pupil health	1,177,440	1,177,966	0.0
2500	Business office	805,331	780,317	−3.1
2600	Plant maintenance	7,789,285	8,400,734	7.8
2700	Transportation	5,695,637	6,583,443	15.6
2800	Central support	509,431	470,754	−7.6
2900	Other support	76,000	81,575	7.3
	Support Services	**$26,830,804**	**$28,573,276**	**6.5%**
3200	Student activities	1,364,046	990,059	−27.4
3300	Community services	17,950	25,500	42.1
	Non-Instructional Services	**$1,381,996**	**$1,015,559**	**−26.5%**
4400	Arch. eng.—improvements	0	0	
4500	Bldg. const.—new	0	0	
4600	Bldg. const.—improvements	0	0	
	Facilities Acquisition	**0**	**0**	
5100	Debt service	6,065,218	6,061,608	−0.1
5200	Transfer funds	0	2,875,131	
5900	Budgetary reserve	2,000,000	1,000,000	−50.0
	Other Financing uses	**$8,065,218**	**$9,936,739**	**23.2%**
Total Expenditures		**$103,000,000**	**$110,390,648**	**7.2%**
Fund Balance—July 1		**$6,496,740**	**$10,800,000**	
Unreserved Fund Balance—June 30		**$4,170,540**	**$5,847,120**	

General Fund Expenditure Budget (by Function and Object)

Function Object	1995–96 Budget	1996–97 Budget	Percent Increase
1100 Regular Programs			
100 Salaries	$39,825,447	$43,006,361	8.0
200 Benefits	10,775,436	10,533,517	−2.2
300 Professional services	43,900	54,250	23.6
400 Property services	97,875	130,852	33.7
500 Other services	11,910	8,500	−28.6
600 Supplies	1,231,147	1,209,302	−1.8
700 Property	529,861	204,731	−61.4
800 Other objects	26,468	28,740	8.6
Total Regular Programs	**$52,542,044**	**$55,176,253**	**5.0%**
1200 Special Programs			
100 Salaries	8,582,672	9,859,292	14.9
200 Benefits	2,516,099	2,690,064	6.9
300 Professional services	1,415,656	1,840,984	30.0
400 Property services	15,250	12,898	−15.4
500 Other services	450,994	478,563	6.1
600 Supplies	133,816	92,901	−30.6
700 Property	66,512	17,889	−73.1
800 Other objects	11,670	2,710	−76.8
Total Special Programs	**$13,192,669**	**$14,995,301**	**13.7%**
1300 Vocational Programs			
100 Salaries			
500 Other services	660,000	595,000	−9.8
600 Supplies			
Total Vocational Programs	**660,000**	**595,000**	**−9.8%**
1400 Other Instructional Programs			
100 Salaries	249,307	89,000	−64.3
200 Benefits	65,258	7,000	−89.3
300 Professional services			
400 Property services			
500 Other services	12,704	2,520	−80.2
600 Supplies			
700 Property			
800 Other objects			
Total Other Instructional Programs	**$327,269**	**$98,520**	**−69.9%**
Total Instructional Programs	**$66,721,982**	**$70,865,075**	**6.2%**

. . .

General Fund Expenditure Budget (by Function and Object)

Function object	1995–96 Budget	1996–97 Budget	Percent Increase
3200 Student Activities			
100 Salaries	$675,220	$745,304	10.4
200 Benefits	96,516	99,051	2.6
300 Professional services	20,580	2,934	−85.7
400 Property services	46,113	8,000	−82.7
500 Other services	235,400	89,795	−61.9
600 Supplies	191,067	32,275	−83.1
700 Property	23,000	0	−100.0
800 Other objects	76,150	12,700	−83.3
900 Contribution	0	0	
Total Student Activities	**$1,364,046**	**$990,059**	**−27.4%**
3300 Community Services			
100 Salaries	0		
200 Benefits	0		
300 Professional services	0		
400 Property services	0		
500 Other services	17,600	25,500	44.9
600 Supplies	350		−100.0
700 Property	0		
800 Other objects	0		
Total Community Services	**$17,950**	**$25,500**	**42.1%**
Total Non-Instructional Programs	**$1,381,996**	**$1,015,559**	**−26.5%**
4000 Facilities			
4400 300 Arch., eng.—improvements	0	0	
4500 400 Bldg. construction—new	0	0	
4600 400 Bldg. const.—improvements	0	0	
Total Facilities	**0**	**0**	
5000 Other Financing Uses			
5100 800 Debt service	2,861,633	2,841,608	−0.7
5100 900 Other financing uses	3,203,585	3,220,000	0.5
5200 900 Fund transfers	0	2,875,131	
5900 900 Budgetary reserve	2,000,000	1,000,000	−50.0
Total Other Financing Uses	**$8,065,218**	**$9,936,739**	**23.2%**
Total Expenditures	**$103,000,000**	**$110,390,648**	**7.2%**

General (Operating) Fund: Detail Expenditure Budget by Function and Object (Instruction—1000 Series)

Account	Budget 1995–96	Budget 1996–97	Percent Increase
1100 Regular programs	$52,542,044	$55,176,253	5.0
1200 Special education programs	13,192,669	14,995,301	13.7
1300 Vocational education programs	660,000	595,000	–9.8
1400 Other instructional programs	327,269	98,520	–69.9
Total Instruction	**$66,721,982**	**$70,865,075**	**6.2%**

Instruction: The activities dealing directly with the interaction between teachers and students and related costs that can be directly attributed to a program of instruction. Teaching may be provided for students in a school classroom, in another location such as a home or hospital, and in other learning situations such as those involving co-curricular activities. It may also be provided through some other approved medium such as television, radio, telephone, and correspondence. Included here are the activities of aides or classroom assistants of any type who assist in the instructional process.

1100 *Regular Programs:* Elementary and Secondary programs include activities designed to provide students (K–12) with the learning experiences to prepare them for higher education and to be productive and contributing citizens in their career pursuits, as family members, and as non-vocational workers, as contrasted with programs designed to improve or overcome physical, mental, social, and/or emotional handicaps.

100 *Salaries:* The funds budgeted here are for elementary classroom teachers, elementary specialists, instructional support teachers, secondary teachers, curriculum coordinators, staff development instructors, teacher aides, and clerical aides. Also included are the budgeted salaries for teachers on sabbatical leaves and their replacements, as well as projected costs of contractual certified credit valuations. Salaries for substitute teachers and aides, whether it be sick leave, personal days, or workshop absences are included here along with stipends for curriculum coordinators, building coordinators, and department chairpersons. All salaries are based on the existing collective bargaining agreement.

Item	Positions	Amount
Elementary classroom teachers	229.0	$16,447,732
Elementary specialists	49.6	3,816,088
Instructional support teachers	9.0	644,440
Secondary teachers	262.3	19,621,366
Career education program	1.0	81,606
ESL program	1.8	146,135
Staff development	1.0	81,606
Teacher induction program		45,059
Curriculum coordinators	4.5	370,604
Curriculum coordinators (EDRPP)		36,806
Curriculum coordinators (summer per diem)		36,018
Curriculum development		69,888
Elem. building coordinators (EDRPP)		69,342
Sec. department chairperson (EDRPP)		100,340
Teacher aides	1.7	28,614
Clerical aides	32.0	468,457
Substitute teachers		454,335
Clerical substitutes		35,970
Lay teachers		6,000
Retirement/cross movement		445,955
Total	**591.9**	**$43,006,361**

. . .

General (Operating) Fund: Detail Expenditure Budget by Function and Object (Support Services—2000 Series)

	Account	Budget 1995–96	Budget 1996–97	Percent Increase
2100	Pupil services	$2,905,109	$3,034,057	4.4
2200	Instruction staff services	2,591,054	2,454,700	−5.3
2300	Administration services	5,281,517	5,589,730	5.8
2400	Pupil health services	1,177,440	1,177,966	0.0
2500	Business services	805,331	780,317	−3.1

(continued)

Account	Budget 1995–96	Budget 1996–97	Percent Increase
2600 Plant operation and maintenance	7,789,285	8,400,734	7.8
2700 Transportation services	5,695,637	6,583,443	15.6
2800 Central support services	509,431	470,754	−7.6
2900 Other support services	76,000	81,575	7.3
Total Support Services	**$26,830,804**	**$28,573,276**	**6.5%**

Support Services: Those services that provide administrative, technical (such as guidance and health), and logistical support to facilitate and enhance instruction. Support services exist as adjuncts for the fulfillment of the objectives of instruction, community services, and enterprise programs rather than as entities within themselves.

2100 *Pupil services:* Activities designed to assess and improve the well-being of students, to supplement the teaching process, and meet the provisions of Article XII of the Public School Code of 1949, as amended. Included are activities designed to provide program coordination, consultation, and services to the pupil personnel staff of the district.

100 *Salaries:* Guidance counselors work with students and parents, provide consultation to other staff members on learning problems, evaluate the abilities of students, assist students as they make their own educational and career plans and choices, assist students in personal and social development, provide referral assistance, and work with other staff members in planning and conducting guidance programs for students. Home and school visitations are done to provide prompt identification of patterns of nonattendance, promotion of improved attitudes toward attendance, analysis of causes of nonattendance, early action on problems of nonattendance, and enforcement of compulsory attendance laws. Psychologists administer psychological tests and gather and interpret information about student behavior. They work with other staff members in planning school programs to meet the special needs of students, as indicated by tests and behavioral evaluation, and plan and manage a program of psychological services for students, staff, and parents.

Item	Positions	Amount
Director of special services	.5	$55,491
Guidance counselors	15.0	1,282,739
Psychologists	7.0	568,177
Social worker	1.0	81,606
Secretarial/clerical	5.5	144,226
Summer per diem		
Guidance		48,943
Psychologist		58,362
Substitutes/overtime		1,800
Federal drug free program		14,000
Total	**29.0**	**$2,255,344**

200 *Fringe Benefits:* Money budgeted for the school district's contribution to the Public School Employees' Retirement Fund and social Security on the above salaries. Also included in this account are the projected costs to provide hospitalization, life, dental, prescription, unemployment compensation, and workers' compensation.

Group health insurance	$151,900
Life insurance	1,719
Disability insurance	2,306
Social security	150,416
Retirement contributions	242,850
Workers' compensation	4,829
Total	**$554,020**

. . .

Capital Reserve Fund Budget

Description	Budget* 1995–96	Budget 1996–97
Revenues		
Interest income	$110,000	$50,000
Donations and contributions		
Total Revenues	**$110, 000**	**$50, 000**

(*continued*)

Description	Budget* 1995–96	Budget 1996–97
Expenditures		
Instructional services		
Regular programs		538,523
Special services		5,594
Support services		
Pupil personnel services		
Instructional support services		408,602
Administrative services	29,135	
Health services		
Business services		
Maintenance services	13,974	4,800
Transportation services		
Central support services		50,154
Building improvement services	2,637,195	1,943,984
Reserve contingency	135,000	350,000
Total Expenditures	**$2,815,304**	**$3,301,657**
Excess Revenues (under) Expenditures	**($2,705,304)**	**($3,251,657)**
Other Financing Sources		
Sale of gen'l oblig. notes—1995	4,000,000	
Sale of fixed assets—Richboro Elem.	401,454	
Refund of prior year's expenditures	500	
Transfers in from general fund		2,506,104
Transfers in from capital projects		2,405,995
Total Other Fincancing Sources	**$4,401,954**	**$4,912,099**
Excess of revenues and other financing Sources over(under) expenditures	**$1,696,650**	**$1,660,442**
Fund Balance—July 1	**$709,345**	**0**
Fund Balance—June 30	**$2,405,995**	**$1,660,442**

*Depicts planned activity from the two Capital Projects Funds.

Capital Reserve Fund Expenditures (by Function)

Function	Description	Budget 1996–97
1100	Regular Programs	
	Equipment	
	120 Replacement computers—elementary schools	$351,675
	36 Replacement computer systems—junior high labs	97,848
	21 Computer systems—junior high science labs	58,800
	13 Computers for ind. arts—CAD program—CRHS	23,400
	2 Computers for ind. arts—photography—CRHS	3,400
	2 computers for ind. arts—graphic arts—CRHS	3,400
	Total Regular Programs	**$538,523**
1200	Special Programs	
	Equipment	
	Computer and printer for learning support—Churchville	1,618
	Computer for emotional support program	3,976
	Total Special Services	**$5,594**
2200	Instructural Support Programs	
	Upgrade library circulation system (59 computers)—CRHS (Partially funded by Federal Grant in General Fund)	408,602
	Total Instructional Support	**$408,602**
2600	Maintenance Services	
	60 Student desks and chairs for 2 new modlars—Richboro	**$4,800**
2800	Central Support Services	
	Development—district-wide area network	50,154
	Total Central Support	**$50,154**
4600	Building Improvement Services	
	Special projects	
	Lighted walkways and canopy for modulars	$51,709
	Purchase 8 add'l. modular classrooms	795,553

(*continued*)

Function	Description	Budget 1996–97
	Replace roof on administration buildings	67,470
	Boiler replacement—Sol Feinstone Elem.	339,400
	Tank removal and new tank installed—Sol Feinstone Elem.	139,495
	Tank removal—administration building	15,574
	Tank removal and new tank installed—high school	131,523
	Tank removal—Newtown Jr. High	80,000
	Replacement doors and windows—Holland Elem.	150,000
	Refurbish canopies—NJHS and RJHS	148,260
	ADA compliance survey	25,000
	Total building Improvement services	**$1,943,984**
5900	**Reserve Contingency**	**$350,000**
	(Additional architect and Engineering fees, and change orders for above projects)	
Total Capital Reserve Expenditures		**$3,301,657**

FUTURE CAPITAL PROJECTS BY COST CENTER

Churchville Elementary

Energy management system installation
Energy efficient upgrades
Sprinkler the boiler room
Sprinkler the stage area
Replace fire alarm detection
Replace two oil burners with gas burners
Resurface parking lot
Replace roof and insulate
Upgrade heating system
Modular roof repairs

Goodnoe/Chancellor Street Elementary

Energy management system installation
Energy efficient upgrades
Sprinkler the storage area
GFCI receptacles at classroom sinks

Update fire alarm misc.
Replace fire alarm detection
Replace boiler near nurse's office (Chancellor)
Alarm system (Chancellor)

Hillcrest Elementary

Energy management system installation
Energy efficient upgrades
Install alarm system
Install backup oil system

Holland Elementary

Energy management system installation
Energy efficient upgrades
Sprinkler the boiler room
Sprinkler the stage and receiving area
Gym folding door second safety control
Replace fire alarm detection
Hook up to municipal sewer
Replace roof and insulate
Remove asbestos in exposed ceiling joints
Replace windows, heating/air conditioning
Shades for skylights

Richboro Elementary

Energy management system installation
Energy efficient upgrades
Alarm system
Install backup oil system

. . .

Council Rock School District Bond Amortization Schedule

Due Date	Maturity	Interest Rate (%)	Interest	Fiscal Total
Series of 1990				
Jan 1 1997	$800,000	6.15	$102,325	$902,325
Jan 1 1998	850,000	6.25	53,125	903,125
Series of 1993				
Jun 1 1997	2,280,000	3.55	80,940	2,360,940
Series of 1991				
Mar 1 1997	140,000	5.90	2,500,343	2,640,343
Mar 1 1998	2,405,000	6.05	2,492,083	4,897,083
Mar 1 1999	3,140,000	6.20	2,346,580	5,486,580
Mar 1 2000	3,335,000	6.30	2,151,900	5,486,900
Mar 1 2001	3,545,000	6.40	1,941,795	5,486,795
Mar 1 2002	3,770,000	6.50	1,714,915	5,484,915
Mar 1 2003	4,015,000	6.60	1,469,865	5,484,865
Mar 1 2004	4,285,000	6.75	1,204,875	5,489,875
Mar 1 2005	3,065,000	6.75	915,638	3,980,638
Mar 1 2006	1,475,000	6.75	708,750	2,183,750
Mar 1 2007	1,580,000	6.75	609,188	2,189,188
Mar 1 2008	1,685,000	6.75	502,538	2,187,538
Mar 1 2009	1,795,000	6.75	388,800	2,183,800
Mar 1 2010	1,920,000	6.75	267,638	2,187,638
Mar 1 2011	2,045,000	6.75	138,038	2,183,038
	$42,130,000		**$19,589,333**	**$61,719,333**

COUNCIL ROCK PERFORMANCE MEASUREMENTS

The information provided in this section is drawn from the yearly follow-up done of each Council Rock graduating class and the PDE Public Dropout Survey. The last three years' studies (1993–1995) support the notion that Council Rock High School enjoys a level of performance second to none.

The PDE dropout surveys for 1993 through 1995 indicate slightly more than 2% dropped out in the last three years. Many of these occurred as a result of moving on to white and blue collar employment. The retention rate for Council Rock students was 98.3% in 1993, 98.12% in 1994, and 97.28% in 1995.

In the area of performance, college board scores in each year are well above the national average.

Year	# of Times Test Taken**	Average SAT Math Scores	Average SAT Verbal Scores	Average SAT Total Scores
1992–93	696	509	448	957
1993–94	709	514	452	966
1994–95	694	514	447	961

The percent of graduates who continue on to higher education remains high and fairly constant. In 1993, 92.3% of the graduates enrolled in some form of post-high school education. Graduates from this class enrolled in colleges and universities in twenty-nine (29) states, the District of Columbia, and two foreign countries. The Class of 1994 showed a total of 89.6% of graduates continued on to higher education. They attended higher education facilities in thirty (30) states, the District of Columbia, and one foreign country. The most recent statistics, for last year's class, reveal 89.2% of graduates enrolling in some further education.

ENROLLMENT HISTORY AND PROJECTIONS FORECASTING METHODOLOGY AND TECHNIQUES

Student enrollment projections are a key factor in budget development. They determine or influence many of the financial estimates that go into the budget, particularly in the instructional area. Most types of personnel requirements are derived directly or indirectly from estimates of the number of students to be served. Allocations of funds for instructional supplies and materials, for example, are made on the basis of projected student enrollments.

In addition, the needs for facilities such as the number of schools or classrooms are calculated using the projected enrollments, as are the level of support services. Other expenditure estimates and certain revenue projections are also directly related to the number of students in the school district.

Enrollment projections are completed annually by the central office. The construction of the budget requires detailed estimates of the number of students to be served in the school district during the upcoming year. These projections are made along several dimensions—district total, school building, grade level, and type of student. The dimensions correspond to the instructional and instructional support programs that the district is planning to provide for its students.

There are several different methods for estimating student enrollments. The method used by the district is the cohort-survival method. this method utilizes

**Some students took the test more than once in their senior year.

mathematical forecasting techniques to project future enrollments based on past trends. However, the basic rationale underlying this extrapolation technique is the assumption that the same conditions affecting enrollment in the past will continue to prevail in the future. This assumption requires careful examination of current conditions to determine variances from past trends. The projections also require validation based on information from other data sources, which include planning commissions, building permits, townships, contractors, and real estate agencies.

A brief description of the cohort-survival methodology and district forecasting techniques follows.

Forecasting Techniques

District enrollment forecasts have been highly reliable over time. The margin of error in forecasts has consistently been less than plus or minus one percent. Thus the district has been able to place substantial reliance on projected data as a basis for budget decisions.

As noted, the primary enrollment forecasting technique used by the district is the cohort-survival method. In this method, each grade level is treated as a cohort and the passage of students from one grade to the next is followed through the school system from year to year. Based on historical validation, the district uses three years of prior data as a basis to project future year enrollments. Over time, the three-year retention ratio has been the most reliable projection technique.

For each year of the past three years, the number of actual students enrolled in each grade level is identified as of October 1. It is important that a consistent date be employed in the methodology. Then a survival rate is calculated for each transition of one grade of students into the next grade in the following year. Using the various rates, an average for each grade-to-grade transition is calculated over the three years.

This method does not trace individual children, it only is concerned with the aggregate numbers in each grade in each year. All of the children in the following grade were not necessarily in the prior grade; transfers into the next grade from outside the school system are common. When more students transfer than leave the school system, the survival rate will be greater than 1.0. The average survival rates are then used to project future enrollments on a grade-by-grade basis. The actual enrollments in each grade during the latest year are multiplied by their respective average survival rates, and the results are the projected enrollments in each grade for the next year.

Projections are also forecast beyond the next year for facility planning. To obtain a forecast of additional years, the same methodology is applied. The same survival rates are used, but the enrollments for the latest projected year are substituted for actual enrollments of the prior year. As with all extrapolation techniques, the cohort-survival estimates become less reliable the farther out they are made.

The projections of kindergarten enrollments present a unique problem in the set of grade level projections. In the cohort-survival method, the projections for a given grade level are based on the students in the previous grade. The entry grade into the school district—kindergarten—has no prior grade or students from which to derive its projected enrollments. In order to obtain this information the district examines live birth rates to determine the beginning school age population. The data, derived has been of significant value for the high degree of reliability achieved in the forecast of enrollments.

Accurate enrollment projections are critical as the School District considers a building program to address consistent high rates of growth in most grade levels. To this end, the District has engaged the services of the Pennsylvania School Boards Association to assist the Board and Administration with this process. In September 1995, a report was issued that projects a 32.4% enrollment growth over the next ten years. This report is currently being updated to reflect actual student enrollment for the 1995–96 school year. It is anticipated that upon receipt of revised projections, the School Board will be able to use these numbers to determine an appropriate course of action to address classroom space needs.

Council Rock Enrollment History Projections (Enrollment History)

School Year	Elementary	Junior High	Senior High	District	Std. Incrs.	Percent Change
1985–86	3,553	2,055	3,293	8,901		
1986–87	4,551	2,193	2,500	9,244	343	3.85
1987–88	4,777	2,237	2,457	9,471	227	2.46
1988–89	4,920	2,283	2,353	9,556	85	0.90
1989–90	5,065	2,314	2,312	9,691	135	1.41
1990–91	5,180	2,378	2,341	9,899	208	2.15
1991–92	5,492	2,384	2,411	10,287	388	3.92
1992–93	5,700	2,450	2,450	10,600	313	3.04
1993–94	5,895	2,576	2,463	10,934	334	3.15
1994–95	6,052	2,678	2,469	11,199	265	2.42
1995–96	6,216	2,759	2,530	11,505	306	2.73

Enrollment Projections†

School Year	Elementary	Junior High	Senior High	District	Std. Incrs.	Percent Change
1996–97	6,436	2,846	2,628	11,910	405	3.52
1997–98	6,610	2,952	2,738	12,300	390	3.27
1998–99	6,632	3,100	2,840	12,572	272	2.21
1999-2000	6,746	3,160	2,931	12,837	265	2.11
2000–01	6,726	3,275	3,029	13,030	193	1.50
2001–02	6,734	3,286	3,183	13,203	173	1.33

†Enrollment projections obtained from report filed by Dr. David W. Davare, Director of Research, PSBA, March 1996. 1996–97 enrollment projections calculated by central office administration. Projections based upon October enrollment totals.

Council Rock School District Personnel Resource Allocations (Position Comparison)

Position FTE	Actual 1993–94	Actual 1994–95	Actual 1995–96	Budget 1996–97
Central office administration	5	7	6	6
Principals/asst. principals	21	21	22	22
Teachers				
Classroom	461.9	473.2	487.2	490.9
Specialists	55.8	61.4	69.6	67.1
Special education	87.76	101.87	124.51	129.4
Guidance counselors	14	15	15	15
Nurses	10	10	11	11
Psychologists	8	8	8	8
Librarians	16.1	16.4	16.8	16.2
Administrative tech support	4	4	4	7
Teacher assistants	33.7	34.2	44.3	55.3
Library aides	15	15	16	15
Staff nurses	5.8	5.8	6.8	6.8
Clerical/recess/caf. aides	58.4	59.8	66.3	61.4
Secretaries	49	49	50	49
Security	3	3	3	4
Maintenance	20	20	21	21
Total FTE	868.46	904.67	971.51	985.1

General Fund Revenue History

Function		1992–93 Actual	1993–94 Actual	1994–95 Actual
	Local Sources			
6111	Current R/E taxes	$53,145,921	$56,614,003	$61,015,618
6112	Interim R/E taxes	951,348	657,221	1,057,168
6113	Public utility realty tax	697,326	741,107	866,940
6114	Payments in lieu of taxes	327	327	327
6120	Current per capita taxes	178,403	182,342	185,753
6141	Per capita taxes	178,403	182,342	185,753
6143	Occ. privilege taxes			53,528
6151	Earned income taxes			3,352,154
6152	Occ. taxes—millage	3,646,556	3,787,329	3,906,855

(continued)

Function		1992–93 Actual	1993–94 Actual	1994–95 Actual
6153	R/E transfer taxes	1,449,072	1,696,485	1,705,280
6400	Tax delinquencies	2,451,348	1,667,403	2,734,803
6510	Interest	832,248	987,781	1,906,937
6700	Student activities	16,525	24,617	23,083
6910	Rentals	1,390	10,450	5,360
6930	Sales of equipment			
6940	Tuition from patrons	59,247	60,304	52,472
6990	Misc. revenues	1,901	5,860	4,067
Total	**Local Sources**	**$63,610,014**	**$66,617,569**	**$77,056,100**
7000	**State Sources**			
7110	Basic instructional subsidy	9,764,231	9,825,211	9,923,526
7160	Tuition (Sec. 1305 and 1306)	79,878	67,172	54,076
7170	Instructional support teams	29,000	29,000	58,000
7210	Homebound instruction	1,097	1,366	1,488
7220	Vocational education	875	187	
7271	Special education	2,747,898	2,914,202	3,331,693
7310	Transportation	1,877,756	1,814,152	2,080,042
7320	Sinking fund payments	848,970	494,728	1,123,233
7330	Mental and dental services	20,820	20,977	22,770
7340	Nurse services	189,746	195,358	202,856
7500	Extra state grants	12,744	1,868	
7810	Social security revenues	1,623,378	1,771,772	1,935,852
7820	Retirement revenues			
Total	**State Sources**	**$17,196,394**	**$17,135,993**	**$18,733,535**
8000	**Federal Sources**			
8513	ECIA—Chapter 1	$318,420	$276,904	$260,133
8560	Fed. block grants—Chapter 2	48,249	45,102	38,903
8570	Eisenhower M&S subsidy			
8670	Drug free schools	41,170	30,831	46,897
8690	Other restricted grants			7,498
Total	**Federal Sources**	**$407,839**	**$352,837**	**$353,431**

(*continued*)

Function		1992–93 Actual	1993–94 Actual	1994–95 Actual
9000	**Other Financing Sources**			
9330	Capital projects fund transfer	582,899		
9370	Trust and agency fund transfer	632	640	816
9400	Sale/loss of fixed assets	247		
9500	Refund of prior years exp.	388,783	75,387	
9610	Receipt from other PA LEAs			
Total	**Other Financing Sources**	**$632**	**$389,422**	**$659,349**
Total Revenues		**$81,214,879**	**$84,495,821**	**$96,802,415**

General Fund Summary Expenditure History (by Function)

Function		1992–93 Actual	1993–94 Actual	1994–95 Actual
Revenue				
6000	Local sources	63,610,014	66,617,569	77,056,100
7000	State sources	17,196,394	17,135,993	18,733,535
8000	Federal sources	407,839	352,837	353,431
9000	Other sources	632	389,422	659,349
	Total Revenues	**$81,214,879**	**$84,495,821**	**$96,802,415**
Expenditure				
1100	Regular education	40,812,610	43,987,068	46,690,724
1200	Special education	9,028,829	9,859,611	11,245,261
1300	Vocational education	655,129	658,936	528,841
1400	Other instructional	298,203	366,231	402,279
	Instructional Programs	**$50,794,772**	**$54,871,846**	**$58,867,105**
2100	Pupil services 2,178,062	2,338,175	2,585,152	
2200	Instr. staff services	1,835,374	2,444,875	2,346,962
2300	Administration	3,931,232	4,731,343	5,085,452
2400	Pupil health	912,823	852,943	915,199
2500	Business office	616,136	649,328	685,717
2600	Plant maintenance	6,301,811	6,811,385	7,014,826
2700	Transportation	4,523,698	4,784,188	5,375,272

(continued)

Function		1992–93 Actual	1993–94 Actual	1994–95 Actual
2800	Central support	85,915	79,409	385,640
2900	Other support	62,835	66,189	79,214
	Support Services	**$20,447,884**	**$22,757,835**	**$24,473,434**
3200	Student activities	1,111,055	1,229,210	1,430,842
3300	Community services	24,643	19,541	26,690
	Non-Instructional Services	**$1,135,698**	**$1,248,751**	**$1,457,532**
4400	Arch. eng.—improv.	0	0	0
4500	Bldg. const.—new	0	0	0
4600	Bldg. const.—improv.	17,558	52,283	1,355,167
	Facilities Acquisition	**$17,558**	**$52,283**	**$1,355,167**
5100	Debt service	1,673,766	994,953	1,469,289
5200	Transfer funds	5,283,696	5,081,553	5,462,710
5900	Budgetary reserve	0	0	0
	Other Financing Uses	**$6,957,462**	**$6,076,506**	**$6,931,999**
Total Expenditures		**$79,353,374**	**$85,007,220**	**$93,085,237**

General Fund Expenditure History (by Function and Object)

Function Object	1992–93 Actual	1993–94 Actual	1994–95 Actual
1100 Regular Programs			
100 Salaries	$31,927,591	$34,700,842	$37,252,514
200 Benefits	7,626,790	7,773,419	7,614,176
300 Professional services	1,322	42,575	60,133
400 Property services	61,566	40,388	59,976
500 Other services	30,822	40,972	72,433
600 Supplies	779,294	821,368	1,030,224
700 Property	348,861	525,734	584,729
800 Other objects	36,364	41,770	16,540
Total Regular Programs	**$40,812,610**	**$43,987,068**	**$46,690,724**
1200 Special Programs			
100 Salaries	5,911,488	6,552,633	7,611,156
200 Benefits	1,405,619	1,530,907	1,608,395
300 Professional services	1,269,743	1,268,005	1,503,351

(continued)

Function Object	1992–93 Actual	1993–94 Actual	1994–95 Actual
400 Property services	5,189	7,669	11,572
500 Other services	379,598	434,148	333,251
600 Supplies	53,520	55,583	110,732
700 Property	3,339	9,557	62,808
800 Other objects	333	1,108	3,996
Total Special Programs	**$9,028,829**	**$9,859,611**	**$11,245,261**
1300 Vocational Programs			
100 Salaries	0	0	0
500 Other services	655,129	658,936	528,841
600 Supplies	0	0	0
Total Vocational Programs	**$655,129**	**$658,936**	**$528,841**
1400 Other Instructional Programs			
100 Salaries	193,009	268,054	301,155
200 Benefits	49,653	66,230	72,485
300 Professional services	36,999	28,856	13,651
400 Property services	0	0	0
500 Other services	0	1,608	13,297
600 Supplies	18,541	1,482	1,692
700 Property	0	0	0
800 Other objects	0	0	0
Total Other Instructional Programs	**$298,203**	**$366,231**	**$402,279**
Total Instructional Programs	**$50,794,772**	**$54,871,846**	**$58,867,105**
2100 Pupil Services			
100 Salaries	$1,647,298	$1,776,805	$2,024,153
200 Benefits	420,098	413,968	426,477
300 Professional services	64,679	72,150	77,267
400 Property services	6,247	10,114	10,355
500 Other services	3,611	5,773	2,067
600 Supplies	34,301	35,117	43,883
700 Property	1,483	18,609	
800 Other objects	345	5,640	950
Total Pupil Services	**$2,178,062**	**$2,338,175**	**$2,585,152**

(continued)

Function Object	1992–93 Actual	1993–94 Actual	1994–95 Actual
2200 Instructional Support			
100 Salaries	1,207,475	1,350,401	1,456,936
200 Benefits	304,583	315,809	307,690
300 Professional services	8,111	21,262	75,296
400 Property services	11,545	15,252	22,389
500 Other services	52,160	54,931	59,303
600 Supplies	125,427	273,105	190,685
700 Property	92,467	82,531	223,296
800 Other objects	33,606	331,585	11,368
Total Instructional Support Services	**$1,835,374**	**$2,444,875**	**$2,346,962**
2300 Administrative Services			
100 Salaries	2,806,302	3,016,750	3,128,795
200 Benefits	624,809	727,139	671,176
300 Professional services	78,252	283,053	348,778
400 Property services	140,500	169,372	201,431
500 Other services	50,573	128,802	90,034
600 Supplies	163,432	222,835	299,972
700 Property	27,179	93,599	178,065
800 Other objects	40,185	89,794	167,201
Total Administrative Services	**$3,931,232**	**$4,731,343**	**$5,085,452**

. . .

General Fund Summary Expenditure History (by cost Center)

Cost Center	1992–93 Actual	1993–94 Actual	1994–95 Actual
Churchville Elementary	$2,092,584	$2,259,023	$2,394,610
Goodnoe/Chancellor	3,284,602	3,543,562	3,766,092
Hillcrest Elementary	1,977,622	2,238,405	2,373,254
Holland Elementary	1,509,130	1,572,910	1,738,673
Newtown Elementary	0	158,596	282,919
Richboro Elementary	1,821,421	2,044,540	2,230,433

(continued)

Cost Center	1992–93 Actual	1993–94 Actual	1994–95 Actual
Rolling Hills Elementary	2,069,840	2,313,299	2,453,590
Sol Feinstone Elementary	2,048,207	2,265,908	2,564,212
Wrightstown Elementary	1,213,467	1,374,555	1,461,021
Holland Junior High	3,825,880	4,315,038	4,758,279
Newtown Junior High	3,734,724	4,091,687	4,296,901
Richboro Junior High	3,322,847	3,500,134	3,795,141
Council Rock High School	12,011,742	12,518,407	13,508,579
District Services	24,375,074	24,656,633	27,693,809
Special Services	8,869,166	9,967,726	11,479,948
District Curriculum	1,029,526	1,164,429	1,263,371
District Elementary	2,947,342	3,116,873	3,160,799
District Secondary	65,581	101,372	139,180
District Library	65,320	53,473	218,557
Career Education	95,920	119,114	127,034
Staff Development	42,707	59,916	104,084
Maintenance	2,542,415	2,891,459	2,916,242
Federal, state, and local programs	408,256	358,562	358,511
Total Expenditures	**$79,353,373**	**$84,685,619**	**$93,085,237**
Fund Balance—July 1	**$1,285,790**	**$3,147,296**	**$2,939,895**
Fund Balance—June 30	**$3,147,296**	**$2,939,895**	**$6,653,074**

• • •

Athletic Fund Budget

Function Object	1992–93 Actual‡	1993–94 Actual‡	1994–95 Actual‡
Revenues			
Admissions	$16,525	$24,617	$23,083
Donations and contributions	0	0	0
Total Revenues	**$16,525**	**$24,617**	**$23,083**

(*continued*)

Function Object	1992–93 Actual‡	1993–94 Actual‡	1994–95 Actual‡
Expenses			
3250 Student Athletics			
330 Other professional services	3,183	3,410	3,958
340 Technical services		11,526	15,726
415 Laundry and linen	22,392	30,525	36,815
430 Repairs and maintenance	13,183	5,641	10,856
450 Construction services			
510 Student transportation	97,225	103,345	123,367
580 Travel	9,101	8,035	9,246
610 General supplies	81,755	93,785	135,147
640 Books		283	41
750 Equipment—new	2,664	3,525	25,305
760 Equipment—replacement	4,149	13,920	42,283
810 Dues and fees	67,661	68,115	80,596
890 Miscellaneous	50	150	360
Total Student Athletics	**$301,363**	**$342,260**	**$483,700**
Excess Revenues (under) Expenditures	**($284,838)**	**($317,643)**	**($460,617)**
Other Financing Sources			
Transfers In	$284,838	$317,643	$460,617
Excess of revenues and other financing Sources over (under) expenditures	0	0	0
Fund Balance—July 1			
Fund Balance—June 30			

‡ Depicts revenues and expenditures as if Athletic Fund existed.

PROJECTION ASSUMPTIONS

Revenue

(1) Real estate assessment values will increase at an annual rate of 2.2%. The projected increases are calculated based on a district projection model that incorporates historical trend data and a forecast of future property activity levels.
(2) Earned Income Tax is projected to increase at an annual rate of 3%.
(3) State support, which includes the Basic Subsidy for Instruction, special education, and transportation will remain essentially constant. The assumption is predicated on the financial condition of the Commonwealth and considerations regarding state equity, which could have adverse consequences for the district.

Expenditures

(1) Salary costs will increase at an annual rate of approximately five percent (5%) per year based on negotiated contracts. The assumption is also based on only moderate increases in professional and support staff to accommodate the projected increase in student enrollment.
(2) Benefits costs are projected to increase at the approximate rate of five percent 5% annually.
(3) Expenditures for contracted services accounted for in purchased professional and technical services, purchased property services, and other purchased services, including such appropriations as transportation, janitorial services, vocational education, and special education, are projected to experience inflationary increases of 3.5% for contracted services.
(4) Expenditures over which the district exercises discretionary control will remain as a constant per pupil expenditure. These expenditures include such items as instructional supplies and textbooks. Funds for the maintenance of plant and equipment will remain constant.

General Fund Expenditure Budget Forecast

		1997–98 Budget	1998–99 Budget	1999–00 Budget
	Revenue			
6000	Local sources	$89,347,148	$94,055,177	$99,305,329
7000	State sources	23,126,097	23,126,097	23,126,097

(continued)

		1997–98 Budget	1998–99 Budget	1999–00 Budget
8000	Federal sources	116,920	116,920	116,920
9000	Other sources	51,050	51,050	51,050
	Total Revenue	**$112,641,214**	**$117,349,244**	**$122,599,395**
	EXPENDITURES			
100	Salaries	67,404,552	70,774,779	74,313,518
200	Benefits	17,016,493	17,867,318	18,760,684
300	Professional services	2,568,020	2,657,901	2,750,928
400	Purchased services	6,009,463	6,219,794	6,437,487
500	Other purchased services	8,621,871	8,923,636	9,235,964
600	Supplies	2,677,651	2,677,651	2,677,651
700	Equipment	489,277	489,277	489,277
800	Other objects	3,109,862	3,109,862	3,109,862
900	Other financing uses	4,744,027	4,629,027	4,824,027
	Total Expenditures	**$112,641,214**	**$117,349,244**	**$122,599,395**
	Fund Balance—July 1	**$5,847,120**	**$5,847,120**	**$5,847,120**
	Fund Balance—June 30	**$5,847,120**	**$5,847,120**	**$5,847,120**
	R/E assessment	$244,056,165	$248,937,289	$253,916,034
	Millage increase	19.13	12.29	13.93
	Total millage	291.89	304	318
	Percent change	7.0%	4.2%	4.6%

School Building Information—Council Rock School District

Building	Original Construction	Additions/ Renovations	Site Acreage	Square Footage	# of Modulars Existing	96–97	Projected Enrollment
Elementary Schools							
Churchville	1959	1964/1971	19.57	63,588	9		852
Chancellor St.	1871	1892/1933	2.49	33,785			238
Goodnoe	1963	1989	14.97	70,617	8		750
Hillcrest	1989		20.01	62,180	7		771
Holland	1965	1966	16.66	53,552	8	1	663
Newtown	1994	1995	97.41	77,725			754
Richboro	1989		37.61	62,180	6	2	824
Rolling Hills	1971		18.08	56,928	10		693
Sol Feinstone	1950	1965/1990	31.71	76,483	2		583
Wrightstown	1958	1960/1964	20.07	30,899	5		308
Secondary Schools							
Holland Junior High	1975		68.11	142,272			986
Newtown Junior High	1954		32.51	133,900	2	5	1,108
Richboro Junior High	1964		38.56	85,440			752
Council Rock High	1969		63.31	349,800			2,628
District Totals			**481.07**	**1,299,349**	**57**	**8**	**11,910**

Council Rock Strategic Plan (1996–97 Budget Proposal)

Strategy Number	Strategy Title	Action Plan No.[§]	Action Plan Objective	Cost
8	Assessment	1 ✓▼	To implement alternative methods of student assessment in all curricular areas as deemed appropriate by curricular committees.	S17,804
8	Assessment	2 ✓▼	To afford staff opportunities as needed to become knowledgeable about alternative methods of student assessment.	$0
8	Assessment	3 ✓▼	To communicate with the community the changes in the student assessment process.	$0
8	Assessment	4 ✓▼	To report on state and national assessments as required by law.	$0
8	Assessment	5 ✓ *	To implement a system of assessing student skills in locating, evaluating, and using information and sources effectively and efficiently to produce specific results.	$0
8	Assessment	7 ✓	To annually review and revise as necessary the district's system of reporting student progress to parents to ensure that it is consistent with the methods of student assessment being used.	$0
8	Assessment	8 *	To implement a portfolio-based assessment system that will serve as a basis for ongoing evaluation.	$3,000
	Action Plan Count	7	Assessment Total Cost	$20,804

[§] ✓ = Ongoing; X = Completed; ▼ = State required; * = New.

Council Rock Strategic Plan (1996–97 Budget Proposal)

Strategy Number	Strategy Title	Action Plan No.§	Action Plan Objective	Cost
6	Career Education	1✓	To implement a district-wide, elementary-level Career Day.	$0
6	Career Education	2 *	To publish sources of career education information available to the staff.	$1,000
	Action Plan Count	2	Career Education Total Cost	$1,000
13	Co-curricular	1 *	To provide students with the opportunity to participate in a computer club.	$5,400
13	Co-curricular	7✓	To provide an opportunity for all students to experience and appreciate the fine arts.	$0
13	Co-curricular	8✓	To provide an opportunity for all students to experience an exposure to the literary process.	$0
13	Co-curricular	11 *	To provide for the process of monitoring and adjusting the co-curricular program.	$0
	Action Plan Count	4	Co-curricular Total Cost	$5,400

Endnotes

1. Ovsiew, Leon and William B. Castetter. *Budgeting for Better Schools*. Englewood Cliffs, N.J.: Prentice Hall, 1960, 23.
2. Hartman, William T. *School District Budgeting*. Englewood Cliffs, N.J.: Prentice Hall, 1988, 7–8.
3. Bennis, Warren. *Why Leaders Can't Lead*. San Francisco: Jossey-Bass, 1990, 18.
4. Cattanach, David L. *The School Leader in Action*. Lancaster, Pa.: Technomic Publishing Co., 1996, 1.
5. Bennis, 25.
6. Graczyk, Sandra L. and Clark Godshall. "Budgeting Advice for Newcomers to Superintendency." *The School Administrator*. Nov. 1996, 36.
7. Galbraith, John K. *The New Industrial State*. New York: Signet, 1967, 36.
8. Castetter, William B. and Helen R. Burchell. *Educational Administration and the Improvement of Instruction*. Danville, III.: The Interstate Printers and Publishers, 1967, 15.
9. Kratz, Robert N. "A Study Comparing District-Level, Long-Range Planning Practices In Selected Pennsylvania School Districts With the Literature of Planning." Unpublished Doctor's dissertation, Temple University, 1971, 16–17.
10. Wildavsky, Aaron. *Budgeting: A Comparative Theory of Budgetary Process*. Boston: Little, Brown, 1975, 253–254.
11. Kratz, 130–131.
12. Hack, Walter G., I. Carl Candoli, and John R. Ray. *School Business Administration: A Planning Approach*. Boston: Allyn & Bacon, 1995, 119.
13. Hack et al., 16–17.
14. Hack et al., 119–120.
15. Jordan, K. Forbis and Teresa S. Lyons. *Financing Public Education in an Era of Change*. Bloomington, Ind.: Phi Delta Kappa Educational Foundation, 1992, 4.
16. Jordan and Lyons, 22.
17. Davidson, Jack L. *The Superintendency—Leadership for Effective Schools*. Jackson, Ms.: The Kelwynn Press, 1987, 155.
18. Davidson, 155.
19. Johnson, Susan M. *Leading to Change: The Challenge of the New Superintendency*. San Francisco: Jossey-Bass, 1996, 63.
20. Thompson, David C., R. Craig Wood, and David S. Honeyman. *Fiscal Leadership for Schools*. New York: Longman, 1994, 322.
21. Johnson, 64.

22. Thompson et al., 308–309.
23. Hartman, 25.
24. Thompson et al., 309.
25. Hartman, 27–28.
26. Thompson et al., 310.
27. Thompson et al., 310–311.
28. Wildavsky, 259.
29. Thompson et al., 311.
30. Hack et al., 140.
31. Hack et al., 141.
32. Thompson et al., 313.
33. Hartman, 38–39.
34. Hack et al., 123.
35. Kratz, Robert N. "Planning a Budget Development Process." *PSBA Bulletin*. Feb. 1985, 12–16.
36. Hack et al., 37–38.
37. Hack et al., 50.
38. Protheroe, Nancy. "Local School Budget Profile Study." *School Business Affairs*. Sept. 1995, 24–32.
39. Protheroe, 26.
40. Protheroe, 25.
41. "Selected Expenditure Data for Pennsylvania Public Schools 1993–94." Pennsylvania Department of Education. Nov. 1995, 46.
42. "Selected . . . 1993–94," 112–113.
43. McGee, William L. and James R. Fountain, Jr. "Managing for Results." *School Business Affairs*. June 1995, 4–15.
44. Thompson et al., 347.
45. *Understanding School Finance*. Harrisburg: Pennsylvania School Boards Association, 1993, 90.
46. Snyder, Bradley J. "Critical Success Factors." *School Business Affairs*. Sept. 1994, 16–21.
47. Hack et al., 81.
48. Hack et al., 81.
49. Hack et al., 82–84.
50. Campbell, Gary. "Drawing the Community Into School District Budgeting." *School Business Affairs*. Sept. 1995, 9–13.
51. Campbell, 9–13.
52. Ridler, George E. and Robert J. Shockley. *School Administrator's Budget Handbook*. Englewood Cliffs, N.J.: Prentice Hall, 1989, 5.
53. Ridler and Shockley, 36.
54. Ridler and Shockley, 36.
55. Ridler and Shockley, 248–250.
56. Jacoby, Michael A. "The Future Demands It Now—Multi-Year Budgeting." *School Business Affairs*. June 1995, 16.
57. Jacoby, 20.
58. Tharpe, Don I. "Commentary." *School Business Affairs*. May 1996, 3–4.
59. Russo, Charles J. and J. John Harris. "Buyer Beware." *School Business Affairs*. May 1996, 17–21.
60. Allen, Ian J. "Unreserved Fund Balance and Public School System Finance." *School Business Affairs*. Oct. 1991, 11.

61. Vidlicka, Sondra R. and William T. Hartman. "How Much Is Enough?" *School Business Affairs*. Feb. 1994, 5.
62. Allen, 15–16.
63. Drucker, Peter. *The New Realities*. New York: Harper Row, 1989, 232.
64. Chubb, John E. and Terry M. Moe. *Politics, Markets and American Schools*. Washington, D.C.: Brookings Institution, 1990, 6.

Glossary

THIS glossary contains definitions of terms used in the budget, and not specifically defined elsewhere, and such additional terms as seem necessary to provide a common understanding concerning financial accounting procedures for schools.

Account Group: These groups account for and control general fixed assets and unmatured principal of general long-term debt.

Accounting System: The total structure of records and procedures which discover, record, classify, and report information on the financial position and operations of a school district or any of its funds or account groups.

Accrual Basis: The basis of accounting under which revenues are recorded when they are levied and expenditures are generally recorded when a related liability is incurred, regardless of when the revenue is actually received or the payment is actually made.

Aid to Families with Dependent Children (AFDC): This is a federal (60%) and state (40%) program which provides direct cash payments to families with dependent children. Both the Chapter I programs and the free and reduced meal programs are available to children from families receiving this aid.

Americans with Disabilities Act (ADA): This is federal legislation which mandates non-discrimination on the basis of handicap or disability and prescribes that services, activities, programs and facilities be accessible to and usable by handicapped or disabled persons.

Appropriation: An authorization granted by a legislative body to make expenditures and to incur obligations for specific purposes. An appropriation is usually limited in amount and as to the time when it may be expended.

Approved Private Schools (APS): These are state approved private Institutions which provide special education programs on a day and residential basis for students whose educational needs cannot be met by either the District or the I.U. given the severity of their handicapping condition.

Asbestos Hazard Emergency Response Act (AHERA): This is a regulation that requires schools to conduct inspections, develop comprehensive asbestos management plans, and select asbestos response action to deal with asbestos hazards.

Assessed Value: This is the value placed on property, both land and building, by the County Board of Assessment Appeals. All counties in the Commonwealth are subject to state statutes governing assessments but each county may establish its own procedures for calculating assessments.

Association of School Business Officials (ASBO): ASBO is a professional association which provides programs and services to promote the highest standards of school business management practices, professional growth, and the effective use of educational resources.

Benefits: Money budgeted for benefits of all paid personnel which includes: retirement contribution, Social Security, hospitalization insurance, life insurance, dental insurance, disability insurance, unemployment compensation, and worker's compensation.

Board of School Directors: The elected or appointed body which has been created according to state law and vested with responsibilities for educational activities in a given geographical area.

Bonded Debt: An obligation resulting from the borrowing of money through issuance of bonds by the school district.

Bond, General Obligation: A written promise to pay specified amounts of money at certain times in the future and carrying interest at fixed rates. The obligation to pay is backed by the taxing authority of the district. The proceeds of bond issues are to pay for capital projects and improvements.

Budget: A plan of financial operation embodying an estimate or proposed expenditures for a given period or purpose and the proposed means of financing them.

Budgetary Reserve: This account is not an expenditure function or account; it is strictly a budgetary account to provide for operating contingencies. Expenditures may not be made against the BUDGETARY RESERVE, but only against the line items which appear throughout the functional appropriations. Whatever may be needed from the BUDGETARY RESERVE may not be used until after transfer from the Reserve to the line items against which the expenditures are to be charged.

Business Services: Those activities concerned with the administering of the district's fiscal and internal functions, the accounting for the district physical inventories, purchasing, storage, and data processing.

Central Support Services: Activities, other than general administration, which support each of the other instructional and supporting services programs. These activities include planning, research, development, evaluation, information, staff, and data processing services.

Community Services: Activities concerned with providing community recreation services to students, staff or community participants. This includes the Community Swim and Recreation Programs.

Comprehensive Annual Financial Report (CAFR): This is the primary vehicle by which the school district reports the results of operations and financial condition of all funds at year end.

Contracted Services: Labor materials, and other costs for services rendered by personnel who are not on the payroll of the school district.

Debt Service: Includes payments of both principal and interest on general long-term debt of the school district.

Elementary: As defined by state practice, expenditures of a school organization composed of the grades pre-kindergarten through grade six (6).

Encumbrances: Purchase orders, contracts, and/or other commitments which are chargeable to an appropriation. Encumbrances are not liabilities and therefore are not recorded as expenditures until receipt of material or service. Encumbrances are used in the accounting records for budgetary control.

Equipment: Expenditures budgeted for the purchase of initial, additional and replacement equipment to be used in the operation of the school district.

Expenditures: These are charges incurred, whether paid or not paid, which benefit the current period.

Federal Sources: That revenue from funds collected by the Federal Government and distributed to school districts in amounts that differ in proportion from those which were collected within such school districts. Examples of this revenue would be restricted or unrestricted Grants-in-Aid such as funds for Handicapped Children, Disadvantaged Children, Vocational Educational, Child Nutrition Programs and Adult Education programs.

Fiscal Year: A twelve-month period of time to which the annual budget applies and at the end of which a local education agency determines its financial position and the results of its operations.

Food Services: This service area includes the preparation and serving of regular and incidental meals, lunches, or snacks in connection with school activities and the delivery of food.

Function: This term refers to an expenditure activity or service area aimed at accomplishing a certain purpose or end; for example, Regular Instruction Programs, Special Instruction Programs, Vocational Education Programs, Instructional Staff Services, and Plant Operation and Maintenance.

Fund: A fund is a fiscal and accounting entity, with a self-balancing set of accounts which are comprised of each fund's assets, liabilities, fund equity, revenues, and expenditures or expenses.

Fund Balance: The excess of assets of a fund over its liabilities and reserves.

Fund Balance Appropriations: Monies appropriated from the district's fund balance to offset the shortfall in expected revenues.

Fund, Proprietary: This fund type accounts for district activities that are similar to business operations in the private sector or where the reporting focus is on determining net income, financial position, and cash flow. The Food Service Fund is a proprietary fund which accounts for all revenues, food purchases, and costs and expenses for the Food Service Program.

Fund, Special Revenue: These funds are maintained to account for the proceeds of specific revenue sources that are legally or administratively restricted to expenditures for specified purposes. These include the Athletic Fund and the Capital Reserve Fund.

Fund Transfers: The transfer of funds from the General Fund to the Capital Reserve Fund, the Athletic Fund and the Food Service Fund.

Government Finance Officers Association (GFOA): GFOA is a professional association of government finance managers. GFOA develops and administers programs and provides services in the areas of research, technical assistance, publications, and career development and training.

Instructional Staff Services: Those activities associated with assisting the instructional staff in improving the content and process of providing learning experiences for students. These activities include library/audio-visual operations, curriculum development, and staff development.

Instructional Support Team (IST): A state supported initiative where a team of school professionals review and discuss a child's learning ad recommend appropriate strategies.

Levy: To impose taxes or special assessments.

Local Sources: That amount of money produced within the boundaries of the school district and available to the school district for its use. Examples of this revenue would be real estate taxes, interest income, rentals and tuition payments.

Mill: Property tax rate per thousand dollars of assessed value. One mill is equal to $1.00 per $1,000 of assessed value. To calculate the tax rate, the total property tax amount levied by the district is divided by the assessed valuation of the taxable property, divided by 1,000.

Object: This term refers to the service or commodity obtained as the result of a specific expenditure; for example, Salaries, Fringe Benefits, Professional Services, Supplies, and Property.

Other Financing Sources: These include funds received from the proceeds from long term debt, receipt of interfund transfers and refunds of prior year's expenditures.

Other Financing Uses: Expenditures budgeted for debt service, payments and transfers to other funds including General Fund contributions to the Debt Service Fund.

Other Instructional Programs: Elementary and secondary programs not included in regular, special, or vocational education. This includes federal programs and Homebound Instruction.

Other Objects: Money budgeted for interest payments on debt service, dues, fees, and memberships in school-related organizations.

Other Support Services: All other support services not classified elsewhere in the 2000 Series.

PDE: Pennsylvania Department of Education

Plant Services: Those activities concerned with keeping the physical plant open, comfortable, and safe.

Pupil Health Services: Activities that provide health services which are not a part of curriculum and instruction. Included are activities that provide students and staff with appropriate medical, dental, and nursing services as required by the state.

Pupil Services: Activities designed to assess and improve the well-being of students, to supplement the teaching process, and meet the provisions of Article XIII of the Public School Code of 1949. This includes guidance counselors and psychological services.

Purchased Professional & Technical Services: Those services provided by independent persons or firms with specialized skills or knowledge. This includes educational services purchased from the intermediate unit or independent providers.

Purchased Property Services: Those services provided by an outside agency, firm, or individual to operate, repair, or maintain equipment, buildings, and sites of the district. Included in this area are utilities such as electricity, water, sewer, and trash/recycling removal.

Purchased Services: Money budgeted for transportation services, tuition to other schools (intermediate unit, private schools, technical school, other school districts), insurance contracts, staff travel, printing of district information, postage, telephone charges and fidelity bonds for tax collectors and district officials.

Regular Programs: Provides for regular education of elementary and secondary students (K-12).

Salaries: This includes gross salary for personnel services rendered while on the payroll of the district.

Secondary: As defined by state practice, expenditures of a school organization composed of the grades seven (7) through twelve (12).

Special Programs: These programs include programs in life skills, learning support, emotional support, autistic support, and gifted support for those students found to be exceptional. It also includes programs purchased from the Bucks County Intermediate Unit, and "approved" and "licensed" private schools to meet the needs of other selected students.

State Sources: That revenue from funds produced within the boundaries of and collected by the state and distributed to school districts in amounts different proportionately from the amounts collected within such school districts. Examples of this revenue would be the basic instructional and operating subsidies, and subsidies for specific educational programs such as Special Education and Vocational Education.

Student Activities: School sponsored co-curricular activities including inter-scholastic and intramural athletics, band, chorus, speech and debate, etc.

Supplies: All items of an expendable nature which are acquired for the operation of the district including supplies, books, and energy utility service for heating and air conditioning purposes.

Support Services-Administrative: Those activities concerned with recommending new policies, administering existing policies, and the developing and implementing procedures in connection with the operation of the school district. It also includes the services of those professional, independent, and separate agencies or individuals that are elected, appointed, or retained to assist in the administration.

Transportation Services: Consists of those activities involved with the conveyance of pupils to and from school, as provided by state law. It includes transportation costs only for trips between home and school.

Underground Storage Tank and Spill Prevention Act (UST): This is a federal program mandating registration, compliance monitoring and regulated removal by certified contractors of all underground fuel storage tanks to protect the public and the environment.

Vocational Education Programs: Activities designed to prepare students for entrance into and progress through various levels of employment in occupational fields such as agriculture, business, distribution, health, gainful and useful home economics, and trade and industry.

Index

About the Author

ROBERT N. Kratz retired from the position of Superintendent of Schools of the Elizabethtown School District in 1993 and is presently teaching educational administration courses for Temple University as well as supervising student teachers for Millersville University (PA). Bob has been a school administrator for more than 20 years, serving as Superintendent at Shippensburg Area School District and Assistant Superintendent in the Radnor School District.

Charles A. Scott, currently Superintendent at the Council Rock School District in Newtown, PA, is well known in the Pennsylvania educational administrator circles. Past President of the Pennsylvania Association of School Administrators, Scotty was Superintendent of Schools in the Upper Merion School District (King of Prussia) for 20 years and in the Township of Ocean, New Jersey Schools for 10 years. Dr. Scott has also been an adjunct professor for Temple University.

Harry T. Zechman, Jr., Superintendent of the Eastern Lebanon County School District (Myerstown, PA), has been a Chief School Administrator for more than 25 years. Serving previously as Executive Director of the Lancaster-Lebanon Intermediate Unit for ten years and as Superintendent of Schools in the General McLane School District (Edinboro, PA), Harry has taught educational administration at both Lehigh University and Temple University.

All three authors hold doctoral degrees in Educational Administration from Temple University.